Thank you to everyone who emailed reviews of the first edition. Here are some of our favourites:

D1558229

"A truly meaningful, well-written book that captures the poetry of living life well, and with grace - I am LOVING it. I read it month by month and it gives me great solace and comfort, especially in those times when I feel I'm drifting away from my centre. It re-connects me to the cycles of nature and gives me a clearer, calmer perspective on what is really important to me. I have recommended this book to everyone I know as an absolutely must have."

Eleanor Scott Wilson

Dramatherapist

"This book is proving to be such a friend! It invites me to play and whisks me into some wild corner of Mother Nature where we wiggle our toes in the delicious mud of what it is to be human. It pokes and prods and lays bare hidden hurts with breathtaking directness, it flips over heavy rocks and chases out secrets with ease. This friend tells great stories and paints powerful images that can leave me in no doubt that I am undone, utterly seen for what I am and I can offer no surprises. What a relief! This book is a travelling companion for life, my own inner self is the landscape we are exploring. It doesn't let me get away with only visiting the pretty bits but while I'm travelling with such an eager and wise guide I find I don't mind the grubby bits so much. It comes laden with gifts, insights that leave you nodding and smiling in recognition, practical tools that make it seem possible to finally integrate the dark and light within and inspiring news of fellow travellers. This book insists on wholeness, shadow and light are all divine in this friend's eyes and if on the way I get all self-pitying this friend will quite rightly push me over in the leaves and flick mud in my hair."

Cate Calder

Cued English tutor, teaching spoken English through vision

"As I read each months' writings I am reminded of ongoing cycles in the natural world and the bigger mythical stage in which the drama of my own process is set. I then feel connected to the landscape and Ian inspires me to go out there, to stalk the wild within and look it straight in the eyes. With the tools and guidance the book provides I am enabled to enter the moment and give voice to what needs to be heard, or enact what needs to be noticed. I recommend this book to anyone who wants to enter the flames of personal therapy, emerge phoenix like and allow the cycle of their lives to move on with greater awareness of, and unhindered by, their past."

Chris Holland

Bushcraft teacher and author of I love my world

"This book contains a gentle yet powerful transformative wisdom informed by the authors' impressive knowledge of ancient lore, nature and the human condition. A fascinating and enlightening read even for the well informed."

Joe Salmon

Director, Tai Chi Nation

2

"Congratulations, and a million thanks for birthing your book 'Eat me'. Aptly named as I devour its contents each month. It has enticed me into the green vein of Nature, to understand more extensively the language of her rhythms and cycles, drawing on tradition, archetypes, metaphors and Earths energies. It is a skillful and poetic guide to transform, heal, and connect us to the relationship between human heart and pulsating planet. My partner has been reading it to me, month by month, how your words wash away the dust on my emotions is nothing short of genius! I beg him to read on, but of course it would be senseless, as it commands the graceful and gentle pace of Nature itself. This book has enlightened, thrilled and floored me. As he reads sometimes all I can do is shout STOP! As I also need the time for it to take root.

Now I have a copy of my own, I will use it as my yearly guide book. I feel you have gifted me with such delicious wisdom, this book now sits in my bag with the rest of my essential items. I can only imagine the labour of love this has been in bringing it into fruition and I can only say on behalf of the feminine, the masculine, and Gaia herself the biggest of Thank yous. You have produced a gem worthy of a best seller."

Catherine Wilcox

Mother, singer, dancer, teacher

"I and my four sisters have had a recent bereavement – we lost our brother, and I bought my sisters your book, we are all finding it poignant, revealing and comforting –especially the parts about grief."

Sharon Hayden

Dramatherapist

If you would like to write us a review or feedback about the book of any kind please visit the web site: www.environmentalartstherapy.co.uk and send us an email.

Environmental arts therapy and the Tree of life

Ian Siddons Heginworth

If you wish to get the most out of this book begin reading it in November and read each chapter in the month of its title. The metaphors, stories and activities contained within relate to our feeling experience of each month and will not make much sense if read out of context.

First edition published by Lulu 2008

Second edition published by Spirit's Rest 2009

Copyright © Ian Siddons Heginworth 2008

Ian Siddons Heginworth asserts the moral right to be identified as the author of this work.

Cover artwork created and photographed by the author.

Front cover: E.A.T. me - Apples, silver birch bark, wire, orchard

Back cover: Lilith - Woodland

To view a gallery of the author's environmental arts therapy images and other related resources go to www.environmentalartstherapy.co.uk

ISBN 978-0-9563863-0-4

Spirit's Rest Books

Exeter

For Marianne
Who makes everything possible

List of contents

Preface

Introduction

About the author

Inspiration

In the silent glades of my heart
I found your footprints again
Shimmering like kisses on the lake's edge
Over mountains of moss they play
Softer than fingertips on a lover's face
And down through the stream
Casting like runes
Wet prints upon stone after stone

Aha, look how you played childlike among the trees
And here in the snow your tracks are crossed by those of wolves and deer
And where you wrestled like bears the earth is black with the soot of your passion

Among the great boulders
Where the ocean stands witness on all sides
I found your shrine
Images of love older than gods chalked upon the milky rocks
The memory of songs still long upon the cry of gulls
And joy, leaping like the whale from the sea's great mouth
Resonant within the womb
Raw and true

Preface

Why in the face of ecological degradation and climate change do we find it so hard, collectively and individually, to act? Why as the wild beauty of the Earth is plundered, sanitized or wiped away do we even struggle to feel our grief at all that we are losing? Is it because the pain of ecocide is so great that the mind can only meet it with denial? Or is it because the abuse and neglect of Nature, the outer feminine, is an outward and cumulative manifestation of our cultural tendency to abuse and neglect the feeling self, the inner feminine?

If so, then we may not be able to truly feel or act on behalf of the outer until we have met and endured the inner. If so, then the maxim "think globally, act locally" has never been more true, but this time the immediate locality is the human heart.

This is a book about the heart and its deep and enduring connection to Nature and her cycles. It is the result of over twenty years working as an environmental arts therapist in therapeutic woodlands around Devon, England. It became apparent that the same metaphors were emerging spontaneously in people's work at particular times of the year and that the Celtic Ogham tree calendar served as an indigenous system of reference for this. I ran an environmental arts therapy course called "The circle of trees" for many years before deciding to put all that I have learned into this book.

But this is not an academic book, neither is it particularly for therapists. Here in the West we live in a culture that over values the masculine - the active, outward part of ourselves that strives and achieves in the world, but under values the feminine - the feeling, inward part of ourselves that receives from the world. Yet so much that is true to ourselves must be felt first by the heart before it can be understood by the mind.

Accordingly, each chapter in this book has a month as its title and should be read in that month to be felt in context with the turning year.

This book is for anyone who loves the human heart and wants to reclaim and honour this long repressed aspect of self. This book is for anyone who loves Nature and wishes to learn a practical ecopsychology whereby the issues that entrap and disempower us can be taken out into the woods, addressed and transformed. This book is for anyone who longs for meaningful ritual and seeks to make it a living part of their lives. This book is for anyone who loves the magical language of metaphor and is beginning to understand its boundless power to manifest change, and this book is for anyone who loves fairy tales, myths and stories and wonders at their possible meanings.

The fairy tale that first truly engaged me was Rumplestiltskin. I played the little man himself in the first play that I ever performed in at primary school. This story has stayed with me all of my life. It speaks about the terrible Faustian deals that we make with ourselves in order to survive in this world. It speaks about a great alchemy, the power to turn straw into gold, that can be granted us and culturally this is an alchemy that we embrace and relish as we transform the wild substance of the world into wealth. But it speaks also of a terrible price, the loss of the first child. The first child is always the inner child. It is this authentic feeling centre, this archetypal totem of freedom, wildness, love, innocence and renewal that we sacrifice over and over again. But the story is not without hope. It tells us that the spell is broken once Rumplestiltskin is named. So it is in our personal therapy that whatever the spell is that binds us, once it is named, once the words that hold the feeling have been spoken and felt to be true, it loses its power over us and things begin to change.

So this is also a book for those of us that seek, both individually and collectively, to name the spell that binds us.

Introduction

There is always a sense of descending into stillness and retreat as we walk together over the hillsides and follow the path down through the trees to the little cabin by the stream. We light a wood burner and make ourselves comfortable. I ask you how you are and you share a little, reflecting on the time you have had since last we met, the things that happened and the feelings that came with them. Some of these reflections hold depth and promise and we take these out into the wood to work with.

Here in this wild and beautiful place we have everything that we need: time, space, intent, materials, silence and privacy. Here everything that you feel within can be given shape and form, voice and dialogue. Here you can meet the forces that rule you, name and break the spells that bind you, share your fears, release your rage, weep your tears and honour your love. We can muster your power and turn it upon all that would oppress and overwhelm you. We can cherish and nurture the child within and cultivate an ever growing sense of the elder that you are becoming. Gently, with the utmost care, patience and compassion we can begin to unveil and heal your wounds. As we do so, everything changes.

There is magic here too. The delicious synchronicities that occur in almost every session to affirm and verify the paths that we are finding. The mystery of wild places unfolding within and around us, the insight that is given time and time again as we realize the meaning of the metaphors that emerge. The crossing of paths as we meet other wild souls in the wood: a fox, a badger, a deer, an owl. And always the poignant and sacred beauty of environmental art and ritual made with reverence and feeling in wild and lonely locations.

Whatever your struggle there is a path that leads through it. For this is environmental arts therapy

Chapter 1   November

F_{airy trails}

Often in November we make fairy trails. These are little pathways leading through the forest, made in miniature as if by fairies. They wind through the dead bracken, clamber over mossy stumps, cross cold little streams, sometimes they even climb trees. They are lovely to make and a wonder to discover. Yet fairy trails, although deliberately and deliciously childish, are also the means to a very adult end. They are mysterious, wandering lines of text written in a language that only the author can read and telling a story that only the author can tell. The story of a life.

What extraordinary and poignant stories we tell when we are invited to write with Nature's pen. Here is a hole in the ground for depression, here an explosion of autumn reds for love. Here is a gateway of sticks that marks a new beginning, here a cold, hard wall of stone that stopped us dead. Here is a new seedling for a baby born, here a grave for a loved one lost. Here is a big stick for violence, here a bed of moss and feathers for a safe and happy home. Each trail unique, bewitching and utterly meaningless to anyone that might stumble across it. But for the person that made it, it may be the first time that they have ever stepped back and shared an overview of their life not based on what they have done but on how it felt. If only our lives were judged in this way. How heroic would the everyday become.

Usually the first thing I notice about these trails is where they begin. Why in all this vast and tumbling wilderness does a life begin here, under this old Beech, next to this little bog, emerging from this rabbit hole or bursting out from a cluster of honey fungus? Often the storyteller doesn't know at first, it just seemed like the right place to start, but when they think about it, it becomes clear. There was something already here when they began. The page that their story was written on was as unique as the tale that it tells.

Nothing is begat by nothing. Each of our stories begin in the middle of someone else's. What's more, because all beginnings are endings too, something must die in the forest to make room for our little saplings to grow. Somebody's dreams, perhaps a career, a sense of freedom, the full attention given to an older sibling or a path yearned for but not taken for the sake of the new baby. This is the nest into which we are laid, feathered with love and grief in varying measures.

The Celtic year follows the natural cycle of growth but does not begin in Spring when life returns. Neither does it begin in January when our calendars start afresh. The Celtic year begins in November when everything around is dying, because this is when the trees drop their seeds and the cycle of growth begins. The trees are also dropping their leaves so the new year is sown in the compost of the old. This teaches us two things. The first is that all life is born in the presence of death, is dependant upon it and sustained by it. So all new beginnings will, if we allow ourselves to feel it, be full of ambivalence because something must be lost as well. The second thing is that nothing just bursts out of nowhere and takes off and away like a hare. All things begin gently with a seed, an idea, a dream, and this must lay dormant and await its proper time and season before it can grow.

So the Celtic year begins with a great celebration of ending and an honouring of the dead, the ancient festival of Samhain (pronounced Souwen) or Halloween. This festival, first condemned by a church intent on replacing its ideologies with its own and then trivialized by commercialism, was once the most sacred event of the year. Apart from marking the end and beginning of the cycle it was also considered the time when the veil between the living and the dead was thinnest and our ancestors stand beside us. Halloween (meaning Holy evening) has been given a bad press. Although its commercial form does serve a purpose with its masks and its costumes in as much as it is the only time of the year when we are encouraged to embrace our cultural and personal shadow, few people take it very seriously. Its cultural association with witches means that many people perceive the traditional event as a kind of black mass or at the very least a suspiciously pagan affair. This is a shame, because its true roots are in Nature and so belong to all of us. Its honouring of death and reconnection with our ancestors are things sadly lacking in contempory Western culture. When such a big hole is left unattended to, it tends to fill up with fear. So ancestors become ghosts and the mystery of death becomes a cold and frightening thing, a subject to avoid, despite it being the only thing in life that any of us can be sure of. Samhain offers us the opportunity to meet death and our ancestors from a place of love and respect. For our children especially this is a great gift because fear cannot thrive in this climate and when we lose our fear of death we can live more fully in each moment.

A celebration for Samhain

We gathered in the old stable, in the centre of which were piles of natural materials, mostly greenery but also clay and wood and someone had brought flowers. I had asked everyone to bring photos of their ancestors: parents, grandparents and beloved elders who were no longer alive. Then we made them little homes and shrines, lit by candles, all around the walls of the stable. We sat before them and honoured them with these words "Elder I honour thee for ...." in soft and reverent voices.

Then we all walked round to visit each others ancestors. It was so beautiful that even the little children were silent and wide eyed. The combination of natural materials with candlelight, love and reverence had made the most exquisite shrines. Despite our long hard cultural separation from the sacred we find it in our hearts so easily when it is inspired by those that we love and honoured with Nature's treasure. Every time I see this it gives me so much hope. It is as if nothing is ever really lost. We just have to remember where we left it.

Then the adults sat holding hands in a circle around the edge of the room and the children made a circle of their own in the middle. I asked the adults to feel the circle of ancestors that surrounded us and to remember how they loved, guided and protected us and still do. Then I asked the children to feel the circle of elders around them and how we love, guide and protect them and always will. These circles go on and on for ever, each enclosing the next, like the rings of a great and boundless tree.

We asked the ancestors to give us their blessing and then asked the children for theirs too. This involved an old tradition of scattering Elder leaves to the four directions. Then we were done. We shared food in the hay barn and then processed out to the field to stand and sing songs around a great fire.

New beginnings

Every month of the year has a lesson to teach us and November's is that new beginnings do not stand alone. Where there is a child there must be a parent. Everything that we are or can become is shaped and influenced by that parenting, especially in the first seven years, and if we seek to understand ourselves then we must understand this. We must, in the fullest sense, honour our parents, both their light and their shadow. We do this by honouring not so much what they did or didn't do, but how it felt.

So where did we begin? Did we begin as an egg in our mother's body or as the seed in our father's? Did we begin as the union of both or before then, as the spirit that chose to inhabit that union and make it its own? Wherever we began we began at our most feminine, our most feeling, raw and sensing, helpless and vulnerable, an open book for the world to write in. All embryos begin as female before there sex is determined and just as the most ancient of trees holds always the sapling it once was at the centre of its rings, so we hold the child feminine, the soft vulnerable feeling self, at the heart of ourselves throughout our lives. It is the part we fear the most in ourselves and love the most in another, our vulnerability, our sensitivity, the garden of our wounds. Our parents are often the first to plant in this garden.

We cannot over estimate the power of the parent to mould its young, nor the softness of the child putty in their hands. Often the mind cannot grasp it because it happened before mind was king, in the days when feeling sat on the throne. But the heart knows; the heart never forgets. The affairs of the heart have to be felt to be understood and those feelings can be buried deep and unknown to us. They have to be mined for, unveiled little by little as they offer themselves up, tear by tear, like gems from the earth.

But where do we look for this treasure? It is here that we need a guide, a pathfinder, someone who can recognize the soft and subtle tracks that feeling leaves behind as it slips through the forest unseen. Someone who has been this way before and who is not afraid. We can find this in a therapist but even they are the outward manifestation of an archetype that we all possess, the inner elder. We go into therapy because our pain summons us to seek the truth. The therapist holds the role of elder, of pathfinder, until we are ready to own it as our own. This elder has always been there, guiding us with their quiet voice, waiting for us to grow into their mantle and become them. Just as the elder holds the child always at its heart so the child is born with the seed of the elder that they will become. It is only a matter of time and our education in elder hood, our apprenticeship as it were, is our life.

Where might this elder lead us? The affairs of the heart belong in the world of the feminine, the feeling self, so they are hard to track in the rush and bustle of everyday life where the tracks go unseen and ignored and are trampled over time and time again. The pathfinder takes us into still and quiet places. The pathfinder knows that feeling is a wild animal and will hide if you chase it. But if we sit in silence and wait and trust, then it may just cross our path.

So the elder wants us to stop, to give ourselves time to feel, and will go to great ends to make that happen. Illness, depression, injury and personal collapse are often seen in therapy to be the means by which the higher self stops us in our tracks and makes us take stock. These are drastic measures made necessary by a cultural ethos that tells us that feeling is irrational, problematic and therefore best avoided. But our elder knows better. If we would listen to them and subscribe to their way then perhaps we would not need to be stopped so dramatically. For we can find the world of the feminine all around us. Nature.

The mirror

When we go with open eyes and a willing heart into Nature we find our inner feminine, our feeling self, reflected. The very face of Nature is a mirror within which we find our heart revealed. This is a mystery that lies beyond such exercises as the fairy trail, where we consciously take what is on the inside and place it on the outside so that we can see and interact with it. That in itself is a wonderful thing but this is something more wonderful still. Only in seeking it do we find it and the more we seek the more we know it to be true. Nature and the feeling self are one. If we listen to the elder, the intuition, that knowing voice within that speaks so faintly and is so easy to ignore, then we will always find our truth. Our own unique truth. We will know it to be true because the strength of the feeling that we find there will tell us so.

Every day I watch intuition guide people through the forest to places of release and healing that they did not know were there. I have watched people witness their family dynamics acted out by tiny creatures in a pool of water, or sculpted by the stones upon the ground. Distinctive trees tell distinctive life stories, from birth among the roots to an unseen future among the branches and all the twists and turns marked upon the way. A deep and cobwebby gash in the trunk for abuse. A flourish of barbed wire overgrown by bark for a time of entrapment. A branch torn away by storms for the loss of a loved one. Beautiful mysteries come to us as well, an eggshell shaken off by an unseen chick in the branches above and landing at the feet of a women who was talking about her new beginning. A deer crossing our path as we reflect on love and gentleness. The haunting hoot of an owl as a secret is at last unveiled.

It is these therapeutic synchronicities that validate our work and strengthen our belief, like signs from the gods. They fill our inner child with wonder and share their wisdom with our elder. They profoundly enhance our connection with Nature as we discover, perhaps for the first time, that we can have a dialogue with her.

Or perhaps not for the first time. Maybe we are not discovering but remembering something that we have forgotten. Certainly our ancestors knew about this mystery and First Nation people today still testify to it. But perhaps each of have also known it in our own lives but let go of that knowledge in the face of reason.

Can you remember how you felt the world as a child, how raw and beautiful was her mystery then, experienced for the first time. Can you remember rolling down hills, jumping in puddles, the smell of the earth, snails in their shells and spiders in the web, the sound of the rain, the games played with your own shadow, daisy chains and stinging nettles, the ants with their eggs, wind you could lean into, autumn leaf mountains and the shapes of clouds. Can you remember how the first art we made was environmental art as we played in the mud and the sand and the snow, made dens for ourselves and our toys? This is how we learn to handle the elements of our being. Our body is our earth and as we build with clay and stone so our body grows. Our feeling is our water and as we dam little streams so we learn to hold back our tears. Our mind is our air and as our shouts ride on the wind we learn how to share our thoughts with others. Our power is our fire and drawn to its flame like little moths we learn how anger burns and love heals.

Where has this child gone? Imprisoned within the rings of the years that have come since, some still marked by the emotional forest fires that wounded and scarred us? Made numb by suffering, by struggling, by routine, by familiarity, by time? Have they gone or are they still waiting, waiting for an elder to gather them up and bring them back into the world? To honour them, cherish them, protect and release them.

Rope swings and dolls

Sometimes we find rope swings in the woods and this is always an invitation for the child to re-emerge.

We have found here how we constantly swing between the wounded child that we were and the archetypal child that we are seeking to manifest. The wounded child reacts to situations and relationships that trigger its fear, subtle transferences that keep us trapped in familiar patterns and sabotage any hope of escape. But the archetypal child is a beacon that is never truly extinguished, our infinite potential for renewal, for wonder and for real and enduring freedom. The rope upon which we swing is our tenuous link to the elder, high up in the branches above. It supports us and allows us to play. Sometimes it wears thin or even breaks and we fall on our face in the mud. At those times we may need another elder, a therapist perhaps, to help us tie up another rope and reinstate our connection. But this is only a temporary state of affairs for our true elder, the one within, never stops watching over us from above.

This connection between the old and the new is rarely felt more keenly than in November when the seeds are sown in the presence of death, in the compost of the old year. Here the elder and the child lie side by side, one on her death bed, the other in her cradle. There is great ambivalence in this, our grief and our hope so united.

This is the beginning of a great alchemy and as in all alchemy we are shown a vision of the gold to come as our hillsides explode into colour and smoulder in the low autumn sunshine like the outspread wings of the phoenix. But this is last year's treasure. Our cycle is just beginning.

Known as the tree of inception or new beginnings, the silver birch, the Lady of the woods, is a tree that the Celtic Ogham tree calendar often placed in November. Believed to stand at the gates of paradise the birch stands now at the gateway to the year, a gateway through which we must all pass, laying down our old selves and bearing the seed of the new. A gateway at which we must grieve for what we leave behind and dream of what we desire to come. There are two such gateways in the year and this one leads into darkness. We stand here now, both as elder of what has passed and child of what is yet to be. The silver birch, the tree of birth and initiation, invites us to midwife our inner children back into relationship with the world.

So this is a good time to make dolls. Dolls can be a gift for the inner child or can represent the child itself. We can make them out of clay or mud, woven grasses or carved wood. We can dress or decorate them with the qualities of the child. We can talk to them, weep with them, make vows of our intent to protect and cherish them. We can rescue them from places of pain or imprisonment and make them safe homes in the woods. We can take them out at night and show them to the stars as new born babies are in some traditional cultures. We can take them home to remind us that the child is always with us and needs our full attention. We can stand at the gateway to the new cycle and be an elder to our child, honouring their fears and committing to carry them safely through and on.

When my daughter was born I witnessed such a rite of passage. Her mother defended their right to a natural birth. I watched her descend into herself, her wild and animal body, gather up the child and birth it herself. I have never seen anything before or since that so evoked the power of the feminine. A deep and instinctive natural process so powerful, so archaic, and yet so fragile and sensitive to outside interference. A rhythm, a pulse, an unfolding, a flowering, as insistent as an express train yet so easy to derail. Once interfered with and lost, so hard to regain. Allowed and supported, the elder and child, tethered together, make their sacred crossing as one.

My own birth was not like this. My mother's womb hemorrhaged and she almost died. It was many weeks before she was well enough to nurse me. All the relationship patterns that I have struggled with in my own personal therapy have inevitably led back to this difficult beginning. So it is that the way we start on our journey sets the pattern of what is to come. This is what makes the beginning so precious and so important to defend.

My mother is very old now and when I see her and my daughter walking together I see the two ends of the fairy trail, the child and the elder, and I see that we begin and end life in our feminine. The feminine is not a thing, it is that which contains the thing. The child is like a container waiting to be filled and it is our responsibility to fill it with love and gentleness. The elder is like a container waiting to be emptied and it is our loss if we do not drink from this cup of experience. Here in the West we are not very good at honouring our elders or harvesting their wisdom. Instead we have a tendency to neglect and abuse the feminine in all of its manifestations. This is at the heart of our malaise.

The garden

The silver birch is often the first tree to colonize the wood and the first to leaf in spring. So it is that all our endeavors begin with the feminine, with our hearts desire. Yet we live in a culture that honours the masculine - doing, thinking, striving, building, achieving. The characteristics of the feminine - being, feeling, receiving, holding, letting go, are often perceived as irrational and are given lesser value. Yet a healthy and equal balance of both is so necessary for our health and well being.

To understand the culture that most of us have been raised in here in the West, we must turn to the myths and stories that lie at its foundation. These creation myths pave the way for what is to come. At the very cornerstone of our predominantly Judeo-Christian culture is the story of Eden. Although generally perceived as a story about two people this is also a story about two trees. We are told that in the garden there grew the Tree of knowledge and the Tree of life and that both grew from the same root. If this story is seen in the context of a human life then the garden becomes the womb, the place of innocence, from which we are inevitably cast out, clothed in skins.

The story tells us perhaps about the development of consciousness within the womb. The two trees become the two halves of the brain, both joined at the same root. The Tree of knowledge becomes the rational enquiring left brain. The Tree of life becomes the intuitive, receptive right brain. The story tells us that innocence is lost when Adam and Eve eat from the tree of knowledge and the spiral of learning begins. So the Tree of knowledge is the enquiring mind and its fruit are the things that we achieve and the impact that we make upon the world. The fruit of the Tree of life is the world's impact on us and its feeling consequences. The story tells us that God kept the way to the Tree of life and placed there an angel with a flaming sword to cut down anyone who passed that way. So it is that life cuts us down again and again as we eat the fruit of the Tree of life and grow from children into elders. It takes a lifetime to truly learn the value and understand the purpose of this. The story tells us that we lose our place in the garden because of our pursuit of knowledge, our relationship with the masculine. This has led to a cultural repression of the feminine in all its guises, from the abuse of women and children and the neglect of the elderly, to the destruction of natural habitats and indigenous populations, and at the heart of all, the neglect and abuse of the feeling self within. A return to the feminine brings us home to ourselves. It is a return to the garden.

In the story God, the elder, walks in the garden. He is there at the beginning and watches over his children even when they have been cast out. They must be cast out because the fruit of the Tree of life cannot be eaten in the womb. Only life will lead us to it, and always through the flaming sword that waits for us at the east of Eden, the right side of the garden. Each time we are cut down we are reborn from this womb and emerge a little wiser, one step closer to the elder that we will become. This is a story of both personal and evolutionary development. This is initiation into elder hood.

If we meet a silver birch tree in the moonlight it makes a shimmering silver trail from the forest floor to the stars. Apart from the beech tree it acts as host to more species of fungi than any other tree, especially the red and white spotted flygaric. Because of these qualities it is often considered a fairy tree. Toadstools are the fruit of decay and our journey on the shimmering trail of our life, up towards the stars, begins with the death of all that came before, the dissolution of the old cycle, the decay of the old way. From the composting of old wounds come the fruits of grief, beautiful, unexpected and mysterious as toadstools, with names like humility, compassion, courage and wisdom. November is a fine month to seek out these treasures as they swell, moist and phallic, within the leaf litter. Delicate puffballs that cough out their spores in clouds of mist. Strong fungal steps that make stairways to the sky of old and dying trees. The shameless stinkhorn, erect and determined with a halo of flies. Toadstools as fine and pale as angels but as deadly as Medusa. Mushrooms plump and fresh and tasty and smelling as good as home baked bread. Little black ash cakes that can hold a spark and keep it alive until your fire is ready to light. What mysteries are these that have arisen like Lazarus from the very face of death?

Lie on the ground in a position that defines your old self and let someone cover you with autumn leaves. It is lovely to lie in the earth like this, fermenting like old fruit. Inhale the ripe, smoky fragrance of autumn. Relax into the tickle of the passing beetle. Listen to the gentle sounds that rise above the stillness, the breeze rustling the leaves upon you, your breath whispering in response. Let yourself descend into the peace of the still and slumbering earth. Be still. There is nothing to do and nowhere to go. Imagine yourself dissolving. Imagine the earth in you breaking down and returning to the soil. Imagine the fire in you smouldering like embers until only ash is left. Imagine the water in you draining away, down to the water table below. Imagine the air in you rising up through the leaves to join the breeze. Imagine only the space where once you lay is left, like a ghost or a fossil imprint of an old abandoned life.

Then when you are ready, rise up gently out of the earth and look down at the empty shape that you have left. When I first did this I saw a gingerbread man and realized that I had been running all of my life because I thought that everyone wanted a piece of me. What is the shape of your old self?

When a child is born it is delivered into the world potentially at the mercy of unconscious parenting. In our first seven years an imprint will be stamped upon us by our parental figures that may take the whole of our lives to reconcile. Lessons in love and its absence, in abandonment, rejection, violence and neglect are woven so deeply into the fabric of our being at a time before words that we can grow into adults oblivious to their weight upon us. Yet their feeling consequences such as a sense of failure, unworthiness, inadequacy and shame can dog our steps always, walking beside us like shadow companions on our journey. Although we may normalize our childhood and seek not to blame our parents for our limitations, we unconsciously re-enact these little betrayals time and time again until the wound is bled, until we understand and own it and can move on beyond it. Until we can respond as adults to the wounding in a way that the child never could.

The turning of the year invites us to descend again and again into the bare bones of our being to meet the child, raw and vulnerable, within. Only by peeling away the layers of our lives and revealing the soft core beneath can we begin to learn about our essential self, the free and powerful spirit that we were when we were born and still are beneath the tangle of the years and their struggles. When the trees drop their leaves they surrender to this process, giving up their dead and releasing themselves from the past. When they drop their seeds they trust to the new, casting out their young on an unknown journey into the future. But there are always a few leaves and seeds that cling to the parent and need to be shaken loose.

Birch brooms and new seeds

Traditionally, birch was used to make brooms, to sweep away the old. It was used to birch criminals and beat the bounds of the parish, driving out evil spirits. It invites us now to name the spells that bind us, the old patterns, the parental legacies, the negative and self destructive beliefs that hem us in and weigh us down and turn our anger upon them, sweeping them away like the autumn gales. It invites us to attend to what we cling to and why.

Clinging to the past keeps us from realizing our fullness in the present. Often there was great sweetness in the old ways and even though the fruit has long since ripened, fallen and decayed, we still cling to its memory and long to taste it again. Hidden beneath memories of great pain and suffering is often a half forgotten moment of absolute tenderness, intense personal sharing or the unspoken alliance of souls meeting in despair. These moments imprint themselves upon the heart and are hard to leave behind. But rebirth requires that we travel light.

Having made images of our old selves upon the forest floor we can make birch brooms and sweep them away. To ritualize the beating or sweeping away of an aspect of the old self is to embody the passing of that aspect. Our anger empowers us and with the enactment of the change comes the change itself. The more fury we can raise the better, for we are the autumn storm that rattles the trees and shakes loose the last leaves and seeds. This is an active and conscious process, so to honour and release the feminine we must engage the masculine, our intent, our action and our power. Here at this gateway we find the silver birch enrobed in both silver bark and golden leaves, the moon and the sun, the feminine and the masculine. She stands as a beacon in space and in time. "Pass this way" she says.

When we have swept the old self away we have a clear space to work with, an empty page to write on. Before there was paper, here in our forests there was birch bark. The name birch is thought to come from the Sanskrit word bhurga which means "a tree whose bark is used to write upon". Birch bark does not rot and so ancient books were written upon it. Now we can use it again to write down our dreams and affirmations for the cycle to come. Then we can tie them to seeds. Perhaps acorns for strength and endurance or hazelnuts for creativity and wisdom. Maybe hawthorn berries for love and an open heart or ash keys for alchemy and transformation. Whatever we choose and whatever that choice means to us we are planting our hopes in the body of the earth, casting them upon the winds or offering them up to the waters. The time of death is a time of dreaming and our wishes, our hearts desires, must be sown as seeds so that they can sleep and begin the process of manifestation from the unconscious to the conscious, from the darkness into light, from the womb of the earth to the first breath of air. All unfolds this way, from the inside out, from intention to actuality.

26

The letting go of leaves is an act of submission to the first cold breath of the winter to come. It is a release of the burden of the year that has passed and a token of trust in what lies ahead. The brightness of those leaves can stand in stark contrast to the gathering greyness of November. They invite us to make art upon the forest floor, images and patterns of self, summoned from within and painted now upon the face of our world. To be met and honoured, interacted with and then left. For the pleasure of the wind. For the goodness of the soil. For the shelter of little souls. They invite us too to unleash our inner children once again in leaf fights, in the building of leaf mountains into which we can run and dive, into the whirling dervish of the leaf strewn Autumn gale. They inspire and inflame us with their colours, calling us to our own fire as we raise the power to burst through this gateway and begin again.

Perhaps the brightest of all is the spindle, its incandescent scarlet leaves like flashes of flame in the Autumn hedgerows. Known by the Celts as the tree of illumination, the spindle represents the lightning flash, that moment of profound insight when we find our sweetness and delight inherent in the here and now. To be completely present in Nature, to have our hearts and eyes opened to her all encompassing mystery, is to see and feel as a child again. This is an enlightenment, the knowledge of the paradise that lingers on the edge of every breath that we take. We knew it as children, we long for it as adults but our clinging to the past and obsession with the future keeps us from it. Sometimes only in the face of death do we find that place again.

Children talk about death all the time. Once I asked children to gather smells in little cups. Autumn is full of interesting smells as the world rots down, and smell is the essence of memory and a rich fuel for the imagination. When they had mixed these smells into perfumes I asked them to decide what creatures had these scents. Then among the trees they built their dens. Quietly we visited each one.

The chocolate fox slaughtered rabbits and coated them with chocolate. The man eating apple had a nest full of human bones. The baby unicorns trapped passers by and devoured their flesh. The fire serpent sprung from its hearth and injected its venom. We met death in every den and the children were thrilled by its presence. All children meet death in their play and their prize for doing so is to be fully alive and present in each and every moment. So childhood seems like an eternity, but as adults we run and hide from death and watch our lives fly by in the process. Our relentless pursuit of an elusive future happiness can end up as a wild goose chase over a blurred terrain of missed opportunities and countless moments of love and beauty that we overlooked because we were too busy or too defended to notice. But we do have a choice. The gateway is open every moment of our lives and paradise grows all around us.

Ritual invites us back into the present. Every ritual is a gateway, marking a place of transition from one reality to the next. The month of November is a gateway into the dark half of the year, with the softness of Summer behind us and the hardships of Winter ahead. In wild places we can find many gateways, both natural and man made. The crook between two boughs of a tree. A hole worn by water in a great stone. A rusty old gate in the woods. These are portals into a new life, waiting to be used. Each invites us to lay down and honour the old, muster our power and step through. This ritual does not in itself reorder the way of things. It simply manifests outwardly and consciously the inner change that is happening anyway. By putting us in touch with our little deaths it welcomes us back to life.

A return to the garden is a return to life in the face of death. It is a return to that that truly sustains and empowers us. When I was a child I spent all my time in the garden. There was a row of silver birch trees in which my brother, sister and I hung ropes and poles. They became our castle. We looked down upon the enemy, the nettles on the compost heap below, and sometimes we would descend and attack them with sticks. I made dens for my action men in the rock garden, built ant islands on trays of water and led expeditions through the shrubbery. Everything I needed was there.

Later as an adult, I worked for many years with people who had profound and complex disabilities. In a world of hardly any speech and limited mobility; intuition and metaphor were all that I could count on. I sought common ground, an area of human experience that was meaningful regardless of skills or needs and found it once again outside the studio doors. On hillsides and beaches, in forests, meadows and gardens. Here again was this synchronistic and spontaneous media, this infinite cupboard of materials, this ever changing canvas. Everything I needed was there.

Now as an environmental arts therapist I lead people into wild places and ask simply "how are you?" As their story unfolds I notice metaphors that have depth, hold feeling or are pertinent to the month that we are in. I follow the scent, questioning, until a hidden vein of feeling emerges.

Then we seek it or make it among the trees, with stone, with wood, with water. There is a dialogue, an exchange, a battle, a revelation. Feeling is released at last. Wounds begin to heal. Things change. Everything we need is there.

If my inner landscape is the same as the outer then all my deepest fears and darkest shadows are out there, waiting for me to confront them, like the nettles on the compost heap below. But so too is my joy, my peace of mind, my transformation and my enlightenment. All waiting in the most unlikely places and the most unexpected guises. This is where our elders are leading us. This is the journey that we have begun.

So as November draws to a close, we plant our seeds of change in the belly of the earth, in the crumbling body of our old lives, and we wait. They will not grow yet. They require a season of stillness, dormancy and descent. And so do we.

Chapter 2   December

Shadows

As the days grow short the shadows creep in. The blanket of leaves grows dark and lies like a shroud upon the cold body of the earth as she draws back her fluids into herself. Winter sucks the life out of the land with a harsh and oppressive hunger, and all that is soft and warm recoils in the face of her advance. The woodland creatures hibernate, sealing up their dens to salvage and sustain the heat in the heart of themselves. They wrap themselves around it and sleep, little pockets of hot life imbedded in the cold clay. Secret dreamers among the black roots, spirits of fur and claw and snuffling snout, cave dwellers, fire keepers, as silent as grubs they hide from winter's fierce and probing tongue.

We too are called upon to descend. Into stillness. Into the heat of ourselves. Into feeling. Yet so often we fear descent and struggle to resist it. We fear the death of what we know, the collapse of all that supports us. We fear the shadows that we meet there.

Birth is a descent. Ejected from the womb, we fall from Grace. Held and nurtured within, all our needs had been met. Love and blood were the same thing. Then suddenly life takes us by the scruff of the neck and throws us into the den. Whether born in tenderness or trauma we are born into a world where nothing is guaranteed, where affection flows hot and cold, an intensely sensual landscape of longing and clinging, love and struggle. Down among the roots where the shadows are we seek out the dark heat of mother, her milk, her skin, her breath, but we may find her teeth there also, and father's too. The heart of the family is a secret place known only to those that are raised there, a place where souls wrangle and compete for warmth and sustenance. A place where great wrongs can be cultivated and great salvation found. This underground kingdom is a deeply unconscious realm, hidden from the sun above and drawing from the great well of feeling below. This is our infancy, so steeped in the unconscious that few of us can remember much about it at all. Yet it is our foundation and whenever we are called upon to descend it is to here that we return.

Each of us at some time in our life, sometimes many, will be so summoned. In the dark transitions of adolescence, Saturn's return, mid life, menopause and old age we are usually called into descent. Again at times of loss, illness or depression we may find ourselves shedding the fragile robes of ego and standing raw, vulnerable and alone before the world. It is the means by which we grow down into ourselves, learn to know ourselves and become fully ourselves and it can rarely be denied. The more we resist it, the more it calls us. It wraps itself around us like chains and pulls us down into the murk. Back into the dens of our past, back into base instincts and desperate needs, back into shadow.

The demands of our culture make no room for this. Descent requires retreat. We cease to be functional in a masculine world. We are no longer productive, useful or efficient. We struggle to stay afloat despite the dreadful undertow. Desperately, we may seek diversions from our feelings, over working, over playing, over anything. Or we may seek solace in alcohol, anti depressants or worse. But these only postpone the inevitable.

Yet every winter, Nature surrenders painlessly to this descent. She follows the cycle of her own being back down into the heart of herself. Of all the lessons she teaches us this is perhaps the most profound, that descent is not to be avoided but embraced. Entered into voluntarily it is a sweet release and the doorway to transformation. It is the death and dissolution of the caterpillar in the cocoon.

At the beginning of December we stand at the entrance to this cave and we feel our fear. A tree that the Celtic Ogham tree calendar often placed in December is the rowan, or mountain ash. Outwardly it can grow on the highest peak but inwardly it is found in the abyss, a manifestation of the Tree of life. Its blood red berries smoulder like embers of hope in the dark of our feminine. On the base of each berry is a five pointed star, a pentagram, the ancient symbol of protection. It is our guardian in the place of shadows.

Judaic mythology tells us that Eve was not Adam's first wife. When God created Adam he also created Lilith who was the exact opposite of Adam but his equal in every way. She was the pure feminine and her power was boundless. She would not bow down to Adam or even to God so she was cast out of the garden into the desert to dwell with demons. Here she became an archetype of the dark feminine, abandoned, wronged, raging.

God then created Eve from Adams rib so that Adam would always be her master. But in her role as wife and mother Eve was not whole. She lacked the wild and independent power of Lilith. It was this that she met in the serpent and it tempted her. It tempts us still. Lilith, we are told, fornicates with demons. So Eve and Lilith are a feminine divided into two great archetypes, mother and whore. Both are troublesome. Mother keeps us as children and the whore evokes abuse. Neither invites us into a healthy and equal relationship with the feminine.

When we are born we arrive with all our potential contained within, like the Rowan within the berry. But as we begin to venture out into the world as toddlers, we meet those forces that would restrict and restrain us and so we tantrum, releasing the terrible wildness of Lilith into the world. In reaction those that have held and cherished us can become dark and vengeful gods that squash our free and fiery spirits with their own indomitable power. As a result we learn to push Lilith down into ourselves, down into the empty deserts of our heart, down into shadow. By the time we are adults we have populated her kingdom with demons, aspects of ourselves that we cannot accept or dare not release. This is what we face when we stand at the entrance to the cave, our own terrible shadow reaching out to us.

The dark feminine is our feeling response to the wounds that make us who we are. It settles in the pits and dungeons of the self, in the harsh and barren wastes within. Only when it breaks out do we name it. In cancer its shadows gnaw at us. In psychosis its voice torments us. In violence and abuse it possesses us and drives us to unforgivable ends. In addiction it binds us with a terrible hunger that must be sated if we are to keep it at bay. When we peer down into these depths and glimpse this behemoth passing beneath we may wonder how we could possibly dare to go near it. Why would we wish to?

The dark feminine is often portrayed as a serpent as in the story of the snake in the garden. In myths and fairy tales the world over we meet these great dragons hiding in caves and wrapped around treasure. This is because much that our Soul longs for, the treasure that will transform, empower and free us, can only be found in Lilith's terrible coils. This is the gift of shadow, our forgotten birthright.

Sometimes in December we work indoors or in caves with our own shadows, cast by candlelight upon the walls. Dancing, writhing spectres as insubstantial as smoke yet bound to us forever. We honour them, negotiate with them, ask them their needs and then stepping into their forms, answer with their voices. We make their treasures, from driftwood, crystals, fossils, bones. Mysterious, archaic and shamanic artifacts, full of power and potential. We gather these up and bring them into the light of consciousness, reclaiming them as our own.

Bodies and graves

Winter is the dead time. The land is stripped down to its skeleton and only the evergreens flesh out the bones. As life retreats into the earth we too are drawn back into our bodies. This is essential for descent, for the body is the vessel of the unconscious. All that we do not want to face in ourselves is held in the body, hidden from the enquiring light of the mind, hidden even from the feeling heart.

Lying on the cold earth, ask someone to outline your shape with whatever is to hand, sticks, stones, moss, shells. Sometimes we use flour, leaving pale and ghostly figures on the ground like the traces of death at the scene of an accident. In a group we can lie tangled up together and the white line will create a single amoebic form that testifies to the existence of the group as a unique and amorphous entity. Spend some time lying within your outline, feeling into your body. Where are the aches and pains, the places of stress or discomfort? What part of your body needs attending to, nurturing or protecting? If it had a voice, what would it say?

Now rise up, out of your outline and using the natural materials all around, make images of the things that you sensed in the places where you felt them. Perhaps swirls of dead grass for the fire in your belly or legs filled with fir cones to show the aching weight of sadness carried on your journey. Maybe holly in the heart for anger or ice in the head for fear. If you wish, focus upon a particular point that needs attention and give it a character, a name, a voice. Embody it, releasing it into the world, move with its intent and speak its truth. Attending to the body and its subtle undercurrents is the simplest and most immediate way to enter the underworld.

Another way in is through visualization. Lying by a fire or under a blanket imagine yourself standing at the entrance to a cave. What can you see? What can you hear? What can you feel? Now call for a guide to come to you. If one does not come, step into the cave and call again. You may be surprised at who or what arrives. It may be a person, an animal, a spirit or anything at all. Let them lead you down into the cave. See what is there for you.

The guide is often in some way connected to the purpose of your descent. Once, working by myself in a cabin in the woods I summoned a guide and a giant appeared with a shrouded face. He led me to a place within myself that held great shame. I began to weep, and feeling the shame intensely, pulled a blanket over my head. Realizing that I had become the giant I reached for a mirror in the cabin and said to him, "show me your shameful face". Then I pulled off the blanket, looked at my reflection and facing my shame for the first time, wept for the man in the mirror.

Returning to the body isn't always easy. We spend so much of our life in our minds that we tend to become resident there and forget that there is anywhere else to be. Certainly in December as the advent to Christmas brings its own demands we may struggle to relax and retreat into ourselves, even though the need to do so is growing within us. In workshops I often begin with a warm up called devolution. We move around the space, stretching, leaping, learning how we feel in ourselves today. Then our arms become heavier, our shoulders hunch and moving now with an ape like gait, we grunt and hoot and beat our chests. Devolving still, we become monkeys in the trees, shrieking and squabbling or grooming one another as we meet. Then we are little mammals, scuttling around on all fours, sniffing each other bodies and then scurrying away. Devolving still, we become reptiles, dragging ourselves around on our bellies with flickering, hissing tongues. Then writhing, flapping fish, our mouths opening and closing as we hang suspended on the ground. Then jellyfish, pulsing, rolling, dancing. At last we are single cells, merging one with the other in the primordial ooze, squelching, gurgling, a bubbling pool of hot and steamy human broth slowly settling into stillness and silence down on the grass. Relaxing, panting, we glow like embers smouldering in Winter's hearth.

We can become more elemental still. The elemental touch is a four stage massage that even children can learn. Working in pairs we take turns to massage the other. The fire touch is hot and furious, a brisk rub down on a cold day. The water touch is soft, slow and flowing, accompanied by the sound of waves. The earth touch is the still, firm hand. Sometimes I ask the person being massaged to give a number between one and ten for each separate earth touch. One for "I don't like that very much", Ten for "Yes, yes, yes!" Gradually as we move from touch to touch we learn where our partners love to be held. Finally the air touch is a fleeting, skimming fingertip caress that barely touches the body, becoming lighter and lighter until it is gone. Movement, stillness, touch and feeling, these are our doorways back into the body.

Even without a partner, we can work with bodies. The dark, wet leaf litter is ideal for making human shapes upon the ground, as is snow, mud or sand. Sticks, shells and stones, driftwood especially, make excellent bones. These can be aspects of self, parts of our personality that are changing now or phases in our life that are passing. This is an opportunity to say goodbye, to honour and release the old self. Or it could be someone else, a parent or beloved other who has died, a lover who has left, a child who has grown up, a sibling or friend who has grown apart. It may be enough just to make a mound to represent a grave, and sit beside it. Or it may be a chance to revisit a last moment with the loved one, or share a final goodbye that never happened. Reaching out and touching the leaf litter hand, our heart wells up again and grief can flow.

This touching is essential, feeling is held in the body so contact is so often needed to evoke it. Sometimes we will not know what the metaphor is until we pick up the stone and feel its weight upon us, stroke the lichen with our fingers and recall the bearded face of a beloved elder, cradle the little stick child and feel its fear and anguish as our own.

Sometimes we may find animal remains, waiting beyond death to work with us. Skulls, rib cages, wings full in feather, little half devoured victims strewn like oracles over the earth. Once, wandering about on a wooded hillside at dusk I suddenly found a demonic face staring at me and recoiled in horror. It was a mummified sheep, half propped up by a hawthorn bush. The next day I returned to that sheep to work with themes of sacrifice and loss. Finally, the work done, I took a spade and buried it.

Stone too is evocative of death, grave stones, standing stones, sacred sites for burial and memorial. By building a relationship with a site we make it especially sacred to ourselves and we bring it back to life. For my stag night I and a group of male friends spent the night by a river next to a stone circle. I took seven small stones with me, each representing something that I loved doing in a group of men. One by one we called in each stone. We made a fire. We shared from our hearts. We swam in the river. We sang together. We drummed and danced and wrestled. We shared a ritual of rebirth, passing through the hole in an ancient birthing stone. Now whenever I return to that circle I do not see a ring of cold stone. I see my sweet brothers standing there grinning at me, full of love and power, alive and everlasting.

Rowan was a sacred tree to the druids. It was used to protect stone circles and way mark lay lines. It was used as a guide in visionary rituals and placed upon graves to help the passage of the spirit. Its red berries were the colour of blood, fire and the heart. As we make our journey down into the cave of our being it is the spirit of the rowan that guides and protects us.

The log jam

When I first went into therapy myself my therapist told me that depression was like a log jam. The only way to shift it would be to work loose one log at a time. Then slowly, things would start to flow again. Now, on the strength of my own experience and that of the people I have worked with, I would say that depression is always a symptom of stuck grief. Because we as a culture do not willingly embrace grief and mourn the deaths, both small and momentous, in our lives, these logs stack up within us until nothing can flow. Grief for the things we could not have, the love that was not given us, for the dreams we never realized or the expectations we could not fulfill. Grief for those that we lost and for what we lost in ourselves. Grief because where there is light there is shadow, where there is love there will always be loss. Grief because we are human and to be human is, sometimes, to suffer. I have never met anyone with depression who cannot be helped by learning to grieve. But to go willingly into grief is an act of great faith and courage. To help someone to do this we must offer them both guidance and safety.

The Florentine poet Dante, in his Divine Comedy, shared his own visionary descent into the underworld. He journeyed down through the seven circles of Hell, each one more terrible than the last, until at last he escaped by finding the original wound, the body of the Devil himself, and climbed out upon it to see the stars again. Alone he would have been lost and at the mercy of the demons there but he had a guide and a protector, the Roman poet Virgil, himself a spirit. Virgil knew the way because he had been that way before. So it is that we can guide and support others as they descend into feeling only if we have done so ourselves. This is the essential initiation of the healer.

Of course no one wants to make this descent. We do so under duress, because we have to, and as we feel ourselves slide it is terrifying. Although such a breakdown is actually a breakthrough, a rupturing of the dam behind which waits a lifetime of feeling, it is perceived by the ego, and often by others, as a devastating personal failure. If we are lucky we have someone to guide us and keep us safe, a friend, a partner, an elder, a therapist. Someone who knows the way because, like Virgil, they have been there themselves. They know intimately the circles of their own personal descent and they are no longer afraid. Without this support we are likely to get stuck. Digging in our heels to stop ourselves falling we find ourselves in one of the circles, enduring some relentless suffering. Physical illness, mental health condition, abusive or addictive behaviour, all these and more can be the woes of spirits stuck in mid descent. Hanging onto torment for fear of what lies beneath. Beneath is always the wound.

It is our resistance that makes it so dreadful. Descent is a natural part of the cycle of the year. If we align ourselves to this and surrender annually to descent just as the year surrenders to winter, then it becomes familiar and no longer a place of dread. Instead it is transformed into a place of release, a cleansing of the slate so that we can begin afresh. It becomes a place of wisdom and surprisingly, a place of love. It becomes an annual initiation into the deep self.

Traditional cultures recognized this and used ritual initiation to mark transitions from one stage of life to the next. Often putting the individual at risk or at least creating the illusion of danger the initiation forces a confrontation with death and leaves the initiate no choice but to surrender to a higher will. It is only when these cultures are deprived of these rituals because they are deemed primitive, superstitious or unsafe, that depression often becomes a feature of people's lives, just as it is a feature of ours.

Environmental arts therapy offers us the opportunity to make ritual a living and evolving feature of our lives again. Because Nature is the only true container for wildness it allows us to release our dark and feeling selves in ways that our culture would not otherwise allow. It shows us again and again that we can survive even the most difficult transitions if only we honour our feelings and surrender our intent. It rewards our courage with astute insights and startling synchronicities. It teaches us faith.

An environmental arts therapy ritual is not something that can be learned like a recipe from a book. It is a unique and unfolding encounter between yourself and the natural world. It can neither be predicted nor repeated, it is improvised moment by moment as are all conversations. A good way to begin is to find a location that is meaningful to you, although often the location finds us. Make art with what you find there in a way that will not cause any harm to the location. Use only what belongs there or will return to the soil and the air. Think less and feel more, let impulse, intuition and instinct guide you. You may not understand what you have done until it is finished or until you interact with it and feel its message. What is needed now? What words or actions are required? What needs to be honoured, released, changed or destroyed? If we trust Nature to guide us in these ways we are never abandoned.

There are many ways to die and be reborn in Nature. I have buried a friend under rocks and watched him re emerge soft and new. We have leapt into icy moorland pools and climbed out with our senses as raw as babies. I have led my wife blindfolded for a day from tree to tree, encountering, embracing, sensing and climbing until in the hollow belly of a Yew she took off her blindfold and wept. Tears for the freedom that she had found in her blindness. Tears for the richness, the innocence and the sensuality of her journey. Tears because it was time to return.

The yew is another tree associated with the cycles of death and rebirth. These beautiful trees with their lush evergreen foliage and poisonous red berries can live for thousands of years. The oldest grow only on undisturbed ground and so most are found in churchyards. There is a Breton legend that their roots reach down into the mouths of the dead.

When my hometown was visited by a family of Native Canadians they were taken to visit an ancient yew in a nearby churchyard. We climbed into its huge and hollow heart and talked about the Romans that were marching across the land when it was a seedling. We stood hand in hand around it and felt our unity. Our visitors shared with our ancestors a spiritual vision of the natural world and a respect for all its mysteries. Who would have thought that this grandfather tree, planted so long ago as the druids were being driven from the land, would outlive the centuries of change, persecution and conflict and one day inspire such unity and witness a return to relationship with Nature.

The fire in the heart cave

Rowan was sacred to Brigantia, the Celtic sun goddess. It marks the journey of the sun, the journey of consciousness, down into its feminine aspect in the underworld where it becomes the fire at the centre of the heart cave. Here the sun sleeps out the long dark nights of winter. While the moon rules above, this inner fire lights our way and in its fires are forged the treasures that we need to grow. So descent is not something to be simply endured so that we can be well again. It is in itself a deeply nourishing and transformative place. It can be a place of absolute stillness, peace, release, deep and profound insight and in its hearth burn the fires of love.

But in our culture it can be hard to allow for this descent at a time when we are compelled to rush around in preparation for Christmas. On one hand there is a real need here, to gather resources to sustain us on our journey down, to prepare for descent so that when all is ready and the work is done we can be still and gather together around the hearth. But there is also the capacity for avoidance, because we are already descending and need to rest into our feelings. This can be a hard and uncomfortable place to settle. The descent of the Winter Solstice is no longer honoured as it once was, and that which we do honour will not serve us as it might.

If gifts are made or gathered from the heart then they become the treasures of the heart cave, symbols of love, growth and sustenance given in the darkest place. They reflect the inner treasures that we find there, mysterious treasures, archetypal, ancestral and often as not neglected or unknown. Only by descending can we glimpse these wonders and reclaim there powers as our own. In the glitter and shimmer of Christmas we share and honour this treasure.

So rowan invites us to become familiar with all that guides and protects us in times of darkness and to reclaim the gifts that we find there. Whatever we call our guiding spirit, our elder, the higher self, our guardian angel, our animal guide or the hand of God, a growing relationship with this nurtures our ability to surrender gracefully to descent. As we trust in the inevitability and rewards of this dark half of the cycle, our faith grows strong around us and we carry the protective spirit of rowan within ourselves. This is why rowan was known by the Celts as the Tree of life, because it is in the surrendering, the letting go to life and its dark transitions, that we are enriched and set free.

This is a good time to work in caves. Sea caves are washed clean by the sea so we can use sand, driftwood, shells, seaweed and stones to make the things in us that are dying and need to be left here in the damp belly of the earth. The ocean will accept and consume our offerings. Caves offer us passage in and out of death, like Jonah's whale they swallow us whole and then regurgitate us on the beach, cleansed and recommitted to our journey.

Land caves, made by the passage of water through limestone, are unchanging environments and we must leave nothing here but our memories. Otherwise our art becomes graffiti. These are sacred chambers, ideal for ritual. Here our media is the body and the voice. Here we can weave stories, sing songs and dance by candle light. As temples of shadow caves invite us to embody those spirits within ourselves that we dare not reveal in the light of day. The wild, the embittered, the corrupt, the devoured, such demons are the companions of Lilith and we can own them here. They were always part of us but only when we deny them in ourselves or project them onto others do they rule or restrict us in their desperation to be free. Embraced, they become part of our fullness, a further depth to our soul, a deeper and richer foundation from which to grow.

Of course we can make things in land caves if we are happy to take them with us when we go. Once we spent a whole day, close to the midwinter solstice, working on the theme of descent. In the morning we worked indoors by candlelight, making maps on the floor of our own personal experiences of descent with stone, crystals, fossils and gems. These extraordinary and deeply moving stories of collapse, despair and recovery unraveled before us, candlelit like shrines to suffering, unique glimpses into a fearful and labyrinthine underworld, stark, sacred, beautiful. Then in a visualization we found the entrance to the cave that called us now, summoned our guides and made our descent, chamber by chamber, down to the heart cave. Here we met the one we were losing. This might be an aspect of self or someone in our life, something poignant that was passing, a death of one kind or another. Whoever or whatever it was, each of us found someone or something there, waiting to say goodbye.

In the afternoon we met up with some caving instructors, were provided with overalls, boots, helmets and lights and gathered at the entrance to a system of underground caves. Here we talked about our inner guides. Then we made our descent. Lined with soft, moist clay the passages unfurled like entrails, or the tunnels of beasts, drawing us deeper and deeper into the flesh of the earth. At each chamber we shared stories from our visualization. Then at last we reached the heart cave, an underground lake. There we made the lost ones out of clay and lit them with candles. I made an image of my son. He and I had often been caving there. Now that he was a teenager it was harder to find things to share and I desperately missed my little boy. I said goodbye to the child down among the shadows where we had played together. Then I blew out the candle.

40

The Babylonian goddess Innana, or Ishtar, made a mythical descent to the underworld. Innana was a goddess of love, fertility and birth, but in that aspect alone she was not whole and she needed to descend to embrace her shadow. In her journey down she had to pass through seven gates, at each gate removing an item of clothing or jewellery. These items were her powers, the forces that sustained and protected her. At last, naked and powerless, she stood before her dark sister, the goddess Ereshkigal, who flayed off Innana's skin and hung her on a meat hook to die.

The descent of Innana portrayed the annual disruption of fertility as the seasons turned and her self sacrifice is echoed all around us as the forests are stripped bare and left to endure the death of winter. When we are called upon in our lives to make such a descent, at times of loss, transition or depression, we too must pass through these gateways, shedding one by one the things that sustain and protect us. Losing a partner, our work, our friends, our identity, our self respect, our sense of purpose, until we too meet our dark and hidden selves and are left hanging, raw and defeated. Only by this pathway can we reach our wound, be born again from it and be made whole.

The rowan has a long association with snakes, serpents and dragons. These guardians and denizens of the hidden realms appear in many myths around the world. In Norse mythology, the World tree Ygdrassil was incessantly gnawed at the roots by the Midgard serpent, a great snake that curls around the Earth, just as our wounds gnaw at us. The Norse thunder god Thor, a god associated with the rowan, went fishing with the giants, hooked this great serpent and pulled it to the surface. So rowan leads us to reveal the wound, to bring its body to the surface into the light of consciousness. The snake is a totem of the dark feminine, the wounded self. It crawls upon its belly and hides in the shadows. It sheds its skin so that it can grow, just as we release layers of feeling, leaving our old selves behind. Each time we do, we grow a little.

The snake is also symbolic of the etheric world, the electro-magnetic currents that lie beneath the illusion of substance. In the land they weave their pathways as ley lines and where they cross, we find ancient and sacred sites. In our bodies, they appear as meridians and their nests are our chakras. The electro-magnetic body is the feeling body, the ever flowing feminine self. It is the receptacle of all that we receive, our Holy Grail. Descent invites us to drink from this well. In doing so we learn that we are not alone.

Our five senses are limited tools and only perceive the gross matter of our bodies. Consequently they cultivate the illusion that each of us is an island. But with stillness, silence and presence, we can go deeper. Here in the underworld our bodies are part of all that is. Here we find that even life and death are a trick of the light, that we are all flickers of the same flame casting shadows on the wall. Here, like the shades in Hades, we are eternal.

In December all life is called upon to share this descent. We too are called into stillness where we can feel our union with all things. Here we begin to understand that the fire that burns within us is all around us too, that Nature and ourselves are one. This is the mystery at the heart of environmental arts therapy and indeed, all ecopsychology. If Nature is an outward manifestation of our feminine self then we can find our feelings outside of ourselves, engraved in the lines of her face, imprinted on the tips of her fingers. She can touch us with ourselves when we are least expecting it.

It is this hidden fire that smoulders always at the heart of our being which we find in the heart cave. It is this that sustains and replenishes us when all else is lost. Without descent we are unaware of it and cling to earthly and transient securities. But descent takes us down to the ground of our being, to our very foundation and there we find the hot flames of spirit burning strong, a candle in the darkness to guide and keep us safe always. There is great reward in this. As we curl around our inner hearth, we become like the hibernating bear, powerful and secure in our great and enduring peace.

The lowest point

And so we reach the Winter Solstice, the deepest, darkest part of the year. Traditionally great fires were lit at this time, outward manifestations of the fire in the heart cave. This is the point of transition. Here we sacrifice our old selves among the flames so that we can rise anew. It was here that Jonah surrendered to God's will, having despaired beyond reason in the hot belly of the whale. The whale, his animal guide, had taken him down to the lowest point. Like Jonah we must often reach the point of absolute desolation, the sure knowledge of our own mortality and the complete surrender of all hope that we can still shape or control our own destiny. Here we transcend the beliefs and intentions of our tender egos and find ourselves bound to a greater plan. In this realization, here at the lowest point, we find the first glimmer of hope again, like the berries on the rowan or the lights on our Christmas trees. So as the Solstice turns, the sun begins to return. Myths all over the world mark this miracle and among them, the story of a child of hope, born in a dark and squalid stable in a bleak and desperate time. Here, the stable is the heart cave. This is the meaning of Christmas, the return of the sun or the solar child, the return of hope and love when all is lost and the lowest point is reached.

The Winter Solstice is the most feminine time of the year and so our celebrations are less about doing things together and more about being together. Often we gather indoors around a fire and turning out the lights, we descend into darkness as one. We huddle under blankets, feeling the warmth of the bodies around us, delighting in the silence, letting go into our breath, the heat of our flesh and our love for one another. Together we wait, here in the darkest place. Hearts beat, eyes close, bodies curl around each other for comfort and reassurance. We are slumbering animals in the den. Then, after a while, a child is sent round with a lantern to light everyone's candles. This is the return of the light. We then take turns to share our treasures: poems, stories, songs and food. These are the delights of the heart cave.

If we allow ourselves our descent and embrace the Solstice, then Christmas becomes once again a magical and soulful celebration. In the commercialism and the panic to get it right we have lost sight of this guiding star. We struggle to avoid the descent by rushing around, spending and consuming. Then when the day comes we collapse into anticlimax. But if we allow the descent first then Christmas becomes, wholly of its own accord, as blessed an occasion as it once was for many of us in the innocence of childhood. Children do not prepare for Christmas, it comes by itself to them and sweeps them off their feet. Honouring Christmas after the Solstice means the giving of gifts when all has been taken, the sharing of love when all else seemed lost. Love is the bedrock upon which all other feelings are laid. When we have raged our anger and wept our tears we always find love to be at the heart of the matter. When the wound has bled it is love that begins to heal.

So descent is a rite of passage, an essential initiation into the secrets of our own being that allows us to be reborn stronger, wiser and more conscious than before. Every time we undergo such an initiation our faith in the wisdom of Nature, both inner and outer, grows stronger and so do we. This faith becomes our protection in all life's challenges and endeavours. It is the source of our courage, the ancestral armour that we wear when we emerge from the cave. It is armour of an altogether different nature than that which we sacrificed in the hidden fires within.

In the story of Innana her release and rebirth was negotiated by her male consort. In the Greek myth of Persephone, when the young goddess was abducted and taken to the underworld, her escape was due to the intervention of Zeus. In the fairy tale Sleeping Beauty, it was the kiss of the prince that awoke her from her hundred year night. These stories remind us that what is missing here in this dark and feminine place is the sun, the positive and supportive masculine, and issues of absent or impotent fathering often arise in people's work at this time. Traditionally holly, a tree that the Celts associated with masculinity, with the wild warrior fire of Midsummer, was brought into the house now and mistletoe too, representing the love of the god Esus, literally his semen. Under this, we kiss. From here, the most feminine point of the year, we summon the masculine. This is why when Christmas climbs down our chimneys we call him Father. Strong, gentle, hairy, benevolent bearer of gifts. We yearn for the return of the king.

Chapter 3   January

The bridge

As the sun returns it reaches across the divide between Heaven and Earth to stir the cold body of the feminine back into life. This return of the king is essential because it is the masculine, the active principle, that must kick-start the inertia for change. But there is new purpose here too, for the king is returning from descent.

When we descend into the underworld at any age it is our dark and wounded feminine that we find there. All those unwanted feelings hung upon the hooks like old coats, many in child sizes, left there since our parents or parental figures began judging and condemning those parts of us that they considered unacceptable, antisocial or just plain challenging. Our masculine selves, the active principle within us that thinks and does, now knows about this abused and imprisoned sister, having embodied her suffering and felt her rage. This knowledge is transformative because he now rallies to her defence. This is why we make New Year's resolutions because we return from descent with a strong sense that something must be done to create change.

The Celtic god hero Bran was the archetypal king. A giant amongst men, he was fearless in battle and was the protector of the Welsh people. He gave his sister Branwyn in marriage to the Irish king, but when Bran heard that she was being treated like a slave he waded across the sea with his army and invaded Ireland. The Irish pulled down the bridge over the river Shannon to stop Bran but he lay his own huge body across it for his army to use. Branwyn was rescued but Bran was mortally wounded in the battle. His head was taken back to the mainland where it prophesised in song as a living oracle for many years. Eventually Bran's head was buried under the site of the Tower of London and his totem birds, the Ravens, are there still, watching over him as he watches over the realm.

Bran's sacred tree was the alder and this is the tree that the Celts associated with the month of January. Known as the king of the waters, the alder is robed in a soft purple sheen at this time of year, the colour of royalty. Its wood grows stronger in water and so like Bran it is used to build bridges. This is the strength that comes from the experience of feeling and it is real and enduring.

The bridge of alder makes the crossing between Bran and Branwyn, masculine and feminine, fire and water. On the masculine side it is the domain of the inner king, the warrior within, whose armour has been forged in the fires of rowan. When we emerge from descent, it is on this side of the bridge that we find ourselves. It must be so because we are approaching the point of conception and it is the king that fertilises the seed.

The domain of the masculine is rarely unfamiliar to us. After all our culture values it above all. It is the world of activity, striving, knowledge, achievement and power. It may seem that it holds all things that we want. Our parents and our schools prepare us for it. They encourage us to compete for and acquire qualifications, status and possessions. These things are perceived as the mark of success and the means to happiness.

It is also the place where we take refuge from the feminine, from our feelings, uncomfortable, intrusive and irrational as they may seem. We stay busy, finding always jobs that must be done, dwelling upon future plans because to be still in the present is unendurable. If we wish to avoid ourselves in this way there will always be more jobs to do.

Yet despite its great furnaces, engines and power stations the domain of the masculine can be a cold place. Each of us may be king of our world but each world is an island. Such lives, although immensely busy, can feel empty and without soul, meaning and purpose. There is no magic, no spirit, no God, no true soul connection with another or with oneself, just the endless tasks to be completed, the boxes to be ticked.

In this cold kingdom, there are colder places still. When our wounds are so harsh that they compel us to run as far from the feminine as we can, then we find ourselves in the dark masculine. There is no heart here and therefore no compassion. Here, the abused can become the abuser. Here, there is only the lust for control and the gratification of our needs. The archetype of the dark masculine is the devil, the shadow that arises when the love of God is obscured. So terrible legacies, both personal and cultural, can be passed on from generation to generation, until someone has the courage to face themselves and stop.

46

Issues of kingship, of control, of power and abuse tend to arise on this side of the bridge. We often meet our fathers here. If mother is earth, then father is sky. He can seem a long way away, unreachable, overbearing, at times thunderous. We may feel that we can get along fine without him, but we never lose the sense of him watching us, the very air that we breathe is his breath and we yearn for the sunshine of his love. He gives us or denies us the spaciousness in which we live and grow. If he was oppressive then we struggle against his weight, stunted and yellow like seedlings beneath corrugated iron. If he was absent then we over run the forest, like brambles or nettles, wild and uncontained. If mother is the soil then father is the gardener. He plants the seeds and then has a responsibility to tend and nurture the garden. If he neglects this, the weeds take hold. This is what husbanding means.

We live in a culture hungry for fathers. No longer the hunter or even the sole provider, no longer the warrior, the storyteller, the keeper of ritual, the means to initiation, many fathers have become emasculated and deroled. They often hover in the background, pottering about in sheds and garages, unable to communicate their feelings without losing their temper, emotionally dependent on their wives and disconnected from their children. Or some rule as ruthless and abusive tyrants, hiding their own wounds beneath an armoury of rage.

In January we feel the harsh, cold shadow of father. The sky can be grey, bitter and oppressive. The wind can be cutting, like cruel and judgmental words. Sleet and hail rain violently down upon us. In the face of his onslaught we freeze. Ice is a metaphor for fear, feeling that is held fast and paralyzed by the absence of love. If he cannot shine upon us, then we too are paralyzed, unable to access our own power and terrified of his. Forever children, we wait for the sunshine that never comes.

Even fathers who have died can remain potent and oppressive forces in our lives, keeping us as children because they retain the throne even in death. A dethroning may be necessary, a ritual confrontation with an image of father in which the truth is finally spoken and our rage released. Then we can take the crown.

Alternatively in some families it is mother who, in the absence of a strong king, has taken on the role of the masculine. Father may be absent or impotent. In which case it is she that we must meet on this side of the bridge. Whoever or whatever we must overcome to realize kingship over our lives, it is within ourselves that the battle must be fought first, even if we are still being actively oppressed by another. The relationship between the abused and the abuser is an unconscious agreement within which one takes the power and the other surrenders it. These patterns are usually established in childhood, when we are too young and vulnerable to contest them. But as adults we can, even though the fear of the contest will remain as great as ever.

The true king

Like Bran, the true king does not neglect or abuse the feminine but strives always to honour and protect her, even at the risk of his own life. He does not frighten the children with his anger but he is clear and strong with his boundaries. He is the sunshine in their lives and they bask in his love, his encouragement and his praise. He protects, admires and cherishes his daughters so that they expect to be so treated by other men and will not accept less. He guides and teaches his sons and wrestles with them too so that they feel their power and his and learn to use and control it with love and respect for the other. He is open with his feelings when it is safe to let go, so his children know his heart and can be open with theirs. But when he needs to be the lion, he is fierce and strong and valiant.

The true king is an archetype and even the best fathers can not be like this all the time. But he dwells within us all and it is to he that we must connect now, not only to father our own children but also to father ourselves, whatever our gender. When the true king is absent we may end up enslaving our feminine, like Branwyn, instead of raising her to the throne where she belongs and whatever we do to the feminine within we do to the outer feminine too. But once the true king returns the feminine can be set free because he makes it safe to do so. If our own fathers have been difficult then we may have little experience of this other version. There may have been other men who shone upon us as we grew, or there may have been moments when we felt this from father. These memories are important to us, because they help us activate and flesh out the true king within. Often it is the fear of the masculine and the power it can use or abuse that can keep us from our own inner kingship. Alder invites us to confront the old kings, the fathers and father figures that we still carry within us and challenge their rule over our hearts. It invites us into relationship with the true king within, to honour his wisdom, his compassion and his power.

Lie somewhere warm and comfortable and close your eyes. Breathe deeper and slower and relax. Imagine walking through a forest on a cold winter's day. What can you see? What can you hear? What can you feel? Now imagine yourself walking down hill to a river. Over the river there is a bridge. This bridge is unique to you so what does it look like? On this side of the bridge a man is sitting by a fire. Imagine walking up to him. Sit beside him and enjoy the warmth of the fire. What does this man look like? Know that he is the king within, however poor, neglected or disheveled he may appear. Spend some time getting to know him. Ask him whatever you will and see what he has for you, or requires from you. Don't forget to thank him. Then, when you are ready, say goodbye and walk back the way you came.

Often we make images of these kings at this time. Once we made only their heads out of clay and hollowed them out to make containers. We decorated them with evergreens, alder cones, shells, feathers and stones. Then we wrote tasks for ourselves, important quests that we wished to embark upon over the next year, on small pieces of paper. These were things that we knew that we needed but would take courage to do, like learning to drive, joining a singing group, speaking our truth to a parent. We rolled each of these up and pushed it into a mermaid's purse. These are the egg sacs of dogfish and I had found a huge cluster of them on the beach the day before. They needed to be soaked to become soft again but then they had made perfect little pouches. These we put into the king's head so that each of us had a head full of mermaid's purses, each containing decrees from the inner king. Over the next year we pulled these out at random and, wherever possible, did as we were told. So like Bran the head of the king became an oracle, guiding us through the year to come.

This is the role of the king, to look down from above like Father Sky and see what is needed for the good of the kingdom. Here is a boundary that needs defending. Here, a task well done that needs to be honoured. Here, a young knight in need of a quest. When the king is locked away in his castle, it is only a matter of time before the kingdom goes to rack and ruin. When the king is ailing, everyone suffers. This is not only true of a family but of ourselves too. When our inner king is not on his throne we depend upon others for guidance, safety and our emotional well being. Our crops tend to fail. Our boundaries are undefended and we may be taken advantage of. Because it is not safe, our emotional rivers can dry up and our hearts become hemmed in with thorns. But when the king returns to his throne, the gardener returns to the garden.

Bridges lend themselves eagerly to environmental arts therapy because they are such potent symbols of crossing. If we find a stream or ditch we can make a bridge easily out of branches or stones. Alternatively we can use an existing bridge. Illustrate this side as your masculine and the other as your feminine. What are the qualities of both? By externalizing these qualities we begin to see what is needed to make the crossing. This almost invariably involves the release of anger.

Lighting the fire

As the sun begins to return it brings with it the promise of the true king. No longer need the fire be hidden beneath the ground, it can arise within and around us now, to melt the ice and unseat the old usurpers. But confronted with January's cold shoulder, finding, holding and feeding this little spark is a quest in itself.

When alder is cut its sap looks like blood. This fiery dye was used to redden the faces of warriors prior to battle. The wood also made a fiercely burning charcoal that could be used to make weapons. So alder was a tree associated with anger and with war.

For the returning sun to awaken the seed it must first break through the cold crust of the earth. This breaking through, this release of power, is also required of us to cross the alder bridge. But power resides in the house of anger and of all the feelings this is probably the most repressed in our culture. We repress it because we believe that it is anti-social and that if we show it then surely we will not be loved. We repress it because our parents used theirs abusively or because it feels so huge within us that if we release it surely it will destroy everything. We repress it because we are frightened of upsetting others or inviting their anger in response.

But our anger is our essential and elemental fire. It is our power to say "No! Stop! Enough!" It draws the line that cannot be crossed. It breaks down the walls that imprison us. It blazes the trail to our dreams. Without it, we are defenceless. With it, we are empowered. It is our birthright, a sword that we are all given to wield. Whether we choose to use it to defend the innocent or slaughter them is up to us.

To raise this inner fire we need the right materials. First we need something to direct our fire at. With whom or what must we get angry? What keeps us from this bridge or bars our way across it? We need to make something that can bear the brunt of our anger, something that can be destroyed. Effigies made from branches, sand or straw can be beaten and demolished with a stick. Walls of stone, logs or brambles can be kicked down or burst through.

Then we need the intent to do so. If our inner king is disempowered then this can be hard to muster. In the face of conflict we may feel weak, tired, confused or paralyzed. We may think of a dozen reasons why not to bother. We may need support from a friend or therapist to overcome this. We need to be reminded constantly of the feminine, soft, vulnerable, undefended and in need of our help. In the face of battle it is here that the king rides up and down the front line, instilling in his men the passion and the valour that they will need to win. We must find this now, in ourselves or in another.

Next we need our truth. How have we been wronged? What do we need to say to the wrong doer? Words of power are the simple truth, not flowery and reasonable, but short, angry and to the point. They convey feelings not explanations. They can be coarse and provocative as they are meant to have impact: "How dare you do this to me!" "You bastard!" "You hurt me!" "Get off me now!"

We need our loud voice too. Anger cannot be whispered, it must be shouted and this frees the power within.

Finally we need our body, for this is where anger is held. Anger comes with a stamped foot, a clenched fist, a pointed finger, a smashed plate, a stab, a kick or an object thrown or broken. Anger demands that the spirit of destruction within us be released. Our culture struggles with this and tends to condemn and divert this destructive urge. But stand in any forest at any time of year and witness the powers of destruction and decay breaking down the old wood to feed the new. Without destruction there is no renewal, no change and no growth. It is this force that we muster now.

I remember once finding a bridge by the sea that had little shelves among its eaves. Using whatever I could find on the beach: bits of crab, dead fish, driftwood, shells and litter I made art upon the shelves to illustrate the shadows that I had to honour in order to make the crossing. But when I was done I still couldn't cross. Only when I had taken a stick and smashed my art to pieces had I honoured it correctly, for the feeling was rage and beneath it lay my power. What hides under your bridge?

It is not just the old kings that we may meet here.Our tendency to repress and demonise our anger creates shadow characters, trolls and ogres that lurk beneath the bridge and threaten to jump out and devour us should we try to cross. These may have evolved from the parental legacy, but are now clearly aspects of self, deformed and twisted expressions of a rage kept tightly bound. When we light the fire, they come out to fight. Like the ogre in the Billy Goats Gruff, they can keep us from the greener grass on the other side. Each time we find the courage to confront them, we grow a little stronger and return next time a bigger Billy goat. As we overcome the ogre his power becomes ours.

This power is the sun's power and now we reclaim it from the shadow just as the sun is reclaimed from the underworld. This is the primal push of the masculine towards life made all the more urgent by the lessons learnt in descent. "You will not do that to me again! I am worth more than that! I will break free!" So the horse kicks open the stable door and runs. The dog rips off his muzzle and barks. The eagle breaks out of his cage and soars.

The apex

The river beneath the bridge is the flow of time. Alder bears last year's cones and the new ones to come on its branches all at once. So we stand also on the bridge between past and future, between the tomb of December and the womb of February. This is the edge between the old year as crone and the new year as virgin, to cross it requires the will and the power to be reborn.

So the resistance that meets us on the bridge can be a clinging to the past, an old loyalty, words left unsaid, pain yet to be honoured. Once we pass the point of conception, we are committed to a new cycle. The relentless passage of time will carry us on and whatever has been left undone will weigh heavily upon us. So here, in service to the king, we are called upon to gather up the weights that would oppress us still and honouring each, one by one, hurl them over the side.

Throwing stones into water, mud, ice or snow is a fine way to release anger. Each stone will have its own weight, shape and quality. Hold and examine it before deciding what it represents. Then hurl it as hard as you can, shouting your words of power. The explosions that they make when they land are surprisingly satisfying.

There is a point somewhere midway in January when the warmth of the returning sun is enough to tip the balance between death and life and in the heart of the seed it's slumbering spirit stirs again. This is the point of conception, the kiss of the prince that wakes the sleeping princess. To stand here at the apex of the bridge balanced between masculine and feminine, past and future, is to stand in a place of equilibrium and well-being, witnessing the present from the standpoint of an oracle. It is at this point of balance that we can see the whole picture, the relentless movement of time through this never-ending moment. This is the power of Bran, the oracular head, who as the bridge between worlds can see all and communicate all. Here we stand upon the single root that feeds both the Tree of knowledge and the Tree of life, and we draw from its source.

This duality is in all things. If we consider the two kingdoms of life, the plants and the animals, we can see that the animal kingdom has essentially masculine qualities in relation to its activity, the imprint it leaves upon the earth and the obvious diversity of its species. The plant kingdom is more often portrayed as feminine, relatively immobile, passive and presenting as vegetation, a single interconnected biomass and land cover. As human beings, we stand at the pinnacle of animal evolution. When we look across the divide it is the trees that grow upon the other peak. We 'do', whilst they 'are', and they are as sophisticated in their 'being' as we are in our 'doing'. When we connect to the trees we begin to bridge the divide. We cross from the masculine to the feminine and learn from them the arts of stillness, endurance, perseverance and growth. They teach us how to be.

Nature seeks this balance and as we move through the year, we swing naturally from masculine to feminine and back again, a pendulum of doing and feeling attuned to the cycles of the moon. Standing in the centre we can begin to see the implications of this.

If nature seeks this balance then she will impose it on all organisms. So we are born with a natural equilibrium already established within us. But as soon as we enter into relationship we begin to merge with the other. Our boundaries fuse and become one and the organism expands to include us both. Now one can become more masculine, and the other more feminine. But the balance only applies when we are both together, and when apart we feel incomplete and begin to need the other. Each of us surrenders part of our wholeness to our partner. We can do this with our siblings, our lovers, our parents and our children. We can do it again and again and again, unconsciously seeking relationships that offer us the missing part.

Also, the family itself is an organism. If the majority within it strive to avoid feeling and live only in their masculine, then natural law will force someone, often the youngest and most sensitive, to carry the feminine for the whole group. So while the others are busy with their heads the little one is left with a heart so full it could burst. No one can express so much feeling, so paradoxically this one may strive harder than any to keep a lid on their passions, often unsuccessfully. This is a terrible and corrosive weight upon a soul. They will often be perceived by the others as over-emotional, ineffective, unstable or even ill. Our mental health services are populated by these sensitive survivors who carry the rage and the grief for so many. But this is also the stuff of poetic passion and artistic genius.

So alder invites us to stand at the apex and witness the balance within ourselves and within the organisms of which we are a part. What of ourselves have we surrendered to siblings, friends or partners? Who carries what for us and what do we carry for them? Sometimes the only way to break free of these unconscious Faustian deals is to leave the organism, the relationship or the family, at least long enough to rebuild our own boundaries and reclaim our missing selves. On the other hand if all parts of the organism are made conscious of the division of goods, then a reallocation can take place. The builder can seek quiet times in which to feel. The feeler can seek the tools with which to build. We can seek wholeness within the relationship and being complete within ourselves, love each other all the more.

Making mobiles

Nothing contemplates balance like a mobile. Tiny, delicate mobiles made from the bones of birds, beech nuts and alder catkins bound with gossamer strands of silver thread. Vast and complex mobiles, turning like solar systems beneath the boughs of great trees, meandering shells and skulls, moss balls, seaweed and holly berries. Stones suspended like pendulums, hovering just millimeters from the ground. Fairy like figures made from lichen and sheep's wool, with real feather wings, dancing like gnats upon the breeze. Individual features, holly leaf eyes, a fir cone nose, a mouth of split bark, all slowly turning within the outline of a face drawn upon the air with ivy. Watching us as we pass.

Make a mobile for yourself and see how your masculine and your feminine hang together. What adjustments are needed to find the place of balance? Or make a mobile for your relationship with another or for your family. Who carries the feeling? Who bears the greatest weight? What must change for the whole to find its equilibrium and grace?

At this time of year when the trees are bare it is common to see clusters of mistletoe hanging like mobiles among the branches. Just as alder is a bridge between fire and water, the moment of conception when the returning sun relights the spark of life in the cold, wet womb of the soil, so mistletoe is a bridge between air and earth. Known as druad-lus or druid's plant it was regarded as the plant that falls from heaven, the semen of God. Its acceptance by the tree was seen as the marriage between Father Sky and Mother Earth. This marriage represents in us the moment when we experience mind and body as one. This moment is profoundly therapeutic and the white berries of mistletoe were known as "all heal". When we see that the mind and body is one thing manifesting in two ways then we open a pathway to the healing of all illness through the unveiling and honouring of personal process. Once we open this bridge, all things are possible. Here at the apex of January's bridge we find this balance too, for the bridge lifts and suspends us for a moment between the earth and the sky.

As we cross we approach the feminine side. This is often less familiar to us. There is greater simplicity here but paradoxically it is harder to attain. This is because it cannot be acquired, it comes by itself when we let go. When we become ill we may find ourselves here. When we fall in love we may again. When we meditate we release ourselves into this place. When we weep we are here. In those moments of joy, grace or bliss we are back again. Whenever we surrender activity, thought and intent and allow ourselves to be ourselves in this moment, we are here.

It is hard to define this in words because a relationship with the feminine is an affair of the heart, not of the mind. The mind cannot grasp it until the heart has felt it. So it is with Environmental arts therapy. How can we adequately define a practice where the main therapeutic media is mystery? Where we rely upon synchronicity to guide us? Where nothing is known to be true until it is felt?

The feminine is not an unfamiliar domain to everyone. Even in our predominantly masculine culture some of us dwell more openly in our hearts and that can be a stormy ride, not least because we will draw the unfeeling and cold hearted to us like moths to a flame. Extremes attract each other as the universe seeks its balance.

Once at a conference in January for providers of rehab and recovery mental health services we made a bridge out of ourselves between two trees, one representing the masculine, the other the feminine and considered where we stood upon that bridge. On reflection it was clear that the majority of service users were struggling to live on the feminine side, trying to cope with rogue passions, sweeping mood swings and paralyzing anxieties. Yet the provision offered in response was traditionally the product of the masculine side: institutional settings, care plans and medication, clinical interventions inspired by a medical model. What was needed to reach across the divide and bridge the gap?

Therapeutic outward bound activity is increasingly proving its value in helping service users back to a place of greater equanimity because it begins in Nature, the standpoint of the feminine, yet it builds and cultivates a healthy masculine by helping people meet their fears and step through them. Environmental arts therapy empowers people by helping them release and harness their anger, honour and move beyond their grief and grow naturally into their truer, stronger selves.

On the other side of the bridge, all creative therapists are required to have regular process supervision in which they honour and release the strands of feeling that connect them to their work and to their clients. Yet rarely is this true of the majority of service providers. Without this services have a tendency to polarize, with provision becoming increasingly clinical and service users unmet in the world of feeling in which they live. The institution can continue the legacy of the family within which the service user carries the feeling and the shadow for everyone. If we are to greet each other in a place of balance then we must be prepared to move closer to the feminine within ourselves and be ready to share that with the people that we care for.

In a greater sense we spend a lifetime crossing this bridge. We eat from the Tree of knowledge first and acquire skills and resources, building the lives that we desire. Then traditionally the second half of life was a time of harvest, contemplation and spirituality where if we are lucky, we learn to let ourselves be.

Perhaps in a greater sense still, an evolutionary sense, all of us are crossing together.

To make the last part of the crossing can be difficult too. It is at this point that we realize what we are leaving behind. Crossing the bridge of alder is a recommitment to growth and change. Not everyone is ready, and everyone's bridge is their own, so we may find that we have to leave someone behind. Or an aspect of ourselves, unsustainable hopes and dreams or a stage of our lives. Again we find that every transition marks an ending. Here in the feminine we will feel it before we see it coming. All we can do is shed the tears and let go.

The king has sown his seed but now his job is done. For a while, he can only step back and trust. The spark of life has been kindled again and now needs to be held in the belly of the earth. Allowed to be. Allowed to grow. For this is the domain of the queen. Life must settle a while in her soft womb in readiness for what is to come.

Chapter 4   February

The womb

As the days grow longer and warmth returns, that which has been frozen begins to thaw and feeling returns to the earth. The month of February begins with the ancient festival of Imbolc. Meaning 'in the belly', Imbolc marks the first stirring of life in the womb of the earth. Dedicated to the goddess Bride, it is the first fire festival of the year. Bride, or Bridie, is the virgin goddess and all brides represent her as they walk towards union with the solar masculine. Hers is the new, soft body of the earth as the water begins to flow again and the soil becomes the womb, dark, moist and enveloping. As she nurses the seed within, it begins to reach out to her.

Mother, my other. When we are in the womb, we cannot tell where we end and she begins. We are one, the seed and the earth from which we spring. When we emerge she is still our whole world, our food and our warmth. She is life's embrace incarnate and our relationship with her underlies all relationships. She is our first lesson in love. She sets the mould into which we pour our expectations for what we receive from the world. If she cherishes us, then we will expect the world to cherish us. If she rejects us, then we will expect to be rejected. Her message to us remains at the core of our being throughout our lives.

The womb is a place of ambivalence. We are ambivalent because we don't want to leave, but we cannot stay. The womb contains us, feeds us and keeps us safe but it also confines and entraps us, and in order to grow, we must break out. We are afraid because we cannot know what lies ahead. This is always so. At any transitional point in our lives, we can no more predict that which is to come than can the child in the womb or the elder on their deathbed. This fear is the ice that must melt so that change can flow.

So as feeling returns we find ourselves again in a womb, but one of our own making. The life that has contained and sustained us until now becomes the soil from which we must spring. Part of us will wish to cling to this. Part of us will need to emerge. In order to grow, we must be prepared to let go.

This is the time to make wombs. Little wombs made from mud and sticks, with soft beds of feather and fur within which to lay the seeds of ourselves. Big wombs of willow, stone, dry bracken and moss into which we can crawl, reclining like beasts in the deep scent of the earth. Shallow holes dug by hand in the ground in which we can bury ourselves like bulbs. Womb shapes on the beach with low sand walls, encrusted with seashell mosaic and made soft with a seaweed duvet. Elaborate nests of sticks upon the forest floor or even in the low branches of a tree, decorated like the homes of bower birds with tokens of our old life, large and strong enough for us to curl up within and doze. Tiny wombs of snowdrop and sheep's wool within which we can secrete little Thumbelina effigies of our inner child, kept safe in a match box and carried in a pocket. Wombs not made but found, dark dens and mossy cradles inviting us to come inside and languish, frail and fetal, in the loving arms of the mother.

A celebration for Imbolc

We gathered in the old stable within a circle of candles. The Christian church celebrates this festival as Candlemass. The candle is the little flame, the first hot sparks of life upon the cold wastes of winter's fading countenance. The snow drop, the crocus, little pioneers of spring, brave and hardy scouts that dare to taste the frost and bring colour and hope once again to the deadlands. I had asked people to bring bags of natural materials and I had brought clay, willow, string and lace.

Using three lengths of weeping willow apiece each of us plaited a braid from Bridie's head. Then we decorated these with tokens to represent the most important feeling events of our lives. A bouquet of baby soft feathers for falling in love. A bundle of bones for divorce. A snail shell for a beloved new home. A fir cone, outspread and empty, for the children left and gone. Each braid upon the head of the goddess a single life woven from love, loss and ambivalence.

Then I asked everyone to lay their braids down upon the floor together to make a single womb shape in the centre of the room. This we did and the nest that we made was rich and heavy with the stories bound within, the lives that had made us who we were, that had shaped and sustained us until now.

While the adults had been weaving their stories the children had worked together to make a little bride. They had made her from clay, with willow hair and a lovely bouquet and dressed her in lace. She was Bridie. They placed her in the centre of the womb and we brought nightlights in and lay them around the edge. Then I asked everyone to suggest something that we could do together to bring life to this womb. We sung and we danced, we stamped and we swayed, we warmed it with our hands and blew life into it with our breath. Then each placed a single candle within it, along with a single word spoken, to affirm that which we would have grow there. The goddess Bride is sacred to wells and springs where we are invited to drink from the waters of life and honour the cycle of loving and letting go. When we meet a goddess in myth or tradition it is our feminine, our feeling self, that we honour.

Then, the ritual complete, we enjoyed our food and wine together while two of our sons entertained us with fire staff and drum, little flames burning brightly on the far edge of winter.

The leap

The tree that the Celts associated with the month of February is willow. Known as the Queen of the waters, the willow is the most feminine of trees. Its Celtic name Saile, means to leap or let go, which is why the leap year falls in February. Willow calls upon us to make this leap, but the only way is to release feeling and so cut the ties that bind us to the past. As we do so, life changes and we surge ahead.

There is great magic in this. We can struggle and strive, seek, grasp and build, but if we are still bound subtly to the past then the chances are that we will not attain our dreams. We can waste a lifetime trying to get there this way. But if instead we isolate the strands of feeling that secure us like anchors to times gone, cut them with our anger and weep the tears that were waiting there, we leap forward and everything changes around us. This is because our natural state is one of flux. Only fear and clinging keeps us from it. This is the power of the feminine, its harnessing of natural transformation as a force that nothing can withstand.

Willow is a tree of love, holding Valentine's Day in the heart of its month. But it is also the weeping willow, the funeral herb, and the tree of grief. It teaches us that love and grief are the two sides of the same coin, and that life is a journey through their never-ending cycles. We cannot know love without knowing grief. Neither can we know light without knowing darkness, rising without falling, nor waking without sleeping. If one cannot exist without the other, then we must learn to grieve in order to learn to love. As long as we fear letting go then we can never surrender fully to the mystery of love.

Once, while recovering from my own mid life descent, I had a dream about a battlefield. The trenches, muddy and devastated, were full of bodies. Slowly I saw men crawling among the dead and then they were climbing out of the trenches. They ran across the mud and someone gathered up a flag. Then they were running up hill and we were in the mountains. There was a swelling of celebration, music was playing and people were dancing. I awoke with a profound sense of victory.

Later that day I visited my mother and, without knowing about my dream, she began to talk about the war that she had grown up in and the loved ones that she had lost. She talked about how so many of her generation were not expected to grieve but were encouraged to keep it hidden inside and keep fighting. She was taught this by her mother who had learned it in her own war many years before.

These generations, so wounded by the cruel abuse of war, bequeathed their legacy to their children. Just as they were the casualties of war many of our generation have been the casualties of an upbringing by adults who had not been allowed their own feelings and consequently were afraid of them. Carrying their legacy into adulthood we stand the risk of passing it on to our own children, along with the misery and illness, literally the dis-ease, that goes with it. When we learn to allow grief its natural flow and rhythm we break this legacy, spare our children, and win a victory in a war that began long before we were born.

The willing embrace of grief as an active and conscious process in our lives is a courageous and transformative leap of faith into the unknown. Grief can feel like an ocean within us and we can deeply fear its release, convinced that should we break the dam our lives will be swept away like so much flotsam. But grief in its natural state does not come all at once and even when induced it can be contained. Every time we are cast out of relationship with another or with ourselves by any kind of ending we are cast again out of the womb, expelled once more from the garden. However positive we feel about the change there will always be grief as well because ambivalence is in everything. When we leave our parental home, however exciting it may be, there will be grief about the loss of our childhood. When we enter into union with another, however in love we are, there will be grief about the loss of independence. When we become parents, however much we adore our children, there will be grief about the loss of freedom and when they grow up, however much we love the adults that they become, we must grieve the loss of the children that they were.

Grief is not just sadness, it is a cauldron of conflicting feelings that make little sense when experienced together but carry our heart's truth into the world when honoured separately. A place for all of these feelings can always be found in Nature for she contains all that is wild and natural. Find or make yourself a womb of some kind. A cave, a hollow tree, a nest or a shelter. State your intent not to leave until the work is done. Enter alone or with a witness, a friend or a therapist. Find a place within for fear, for guilt, for anger, for sadness and for love. Begin with fear because fear always sits on top like ice. When we bring it into consciousness it begins to thaw and release the feeling held beneath. Place your hand in the place of fear and speak all your fears in relation to the one you are grieving. Speak it to them, even if they are an aspect of yourself. "I am afraid I will never recover from this. I am afraid I will never love again. I am afraid to be alone" and so on until all your fears have been spoken. Then move to guilt and placing your hand there tell them everything that you feel guilty about. Guilt can be real and tormenting, nursing a pressing need for confession and self forgiveness, but it can also be a great self deception, keeping us from our anger by turning it upon ourselves. When we release it we may begin to feel the resentment smouldering beneath.

The place of anger needs more than words. Pound the ground, break sticks, smash stones or rip ivy from a tree. Use the voice. Remember that the place of love is somewhere else and is safe and unaffected by this. Let all the anger come out, however unreasonable it seems. "How could you die and leave me now? I hate you because I love you and you are gone! You didn't give me a chance to say goodbye! " Let it blaze, that mountain of dead wood that you carry inside, until all has burned away, until only ashes are left.

Anger protects the wound, when it is released the tears can flow. In the place of sadness we honour the lost with our tears. Seek the words that evoke them. Tears are the river upon which our sorrow is carried out of our body and into the world, back into the cycle of water in which it belongs. There is no release from grief without them, so always, always seek your tears.

Finally when all the tears that are waiting have been wept, go to the place of love, the heart of the matter, and speak to the lost one from this place. Love is the heart-stone in the fruit of the tree of life. When we have eaten this fruit, as we must whenever life cuts us down, we need this seed to grow again.

This is a powerful ritual, no less for the person who is called upon to witness it. If it is you, remain silent as much as possible but let your presence be felt throughout. This is an important lesson in how to be with another's feelings. Never try to make it better. Reason or reassurance only blocks or trivializes the experience of feeling, and comes from your discomfort, not theirs. Honour the feelings that come, however irrational they may seem, for this is a place of heart, not mind. Speak only to encourage the expression of feeling if the other is stuck or to share your empathy when your heart is touched. Just a simple word, such as yes or no, is usually enough to convey this. Never try to guess what the feelings are and encourage the other to express them, this is not your heart and you cannot know the mystery of another's. Your presence there is a gift of trust to you and a gift of love to the other.

Another tree that reminds me of grief is the horse chestnut. These trees can grow to a colossal size and the very old ones often look as if they have been in the wars with great branches torn off by their own weight and gaping splits in their bodies. So huge and yet so wounded, these trees command respect and reverence and so does grief. Like grief the fruit of the horse chestnut is not easy to harvest. It comes in an angry and spiny shell that can only be opened by gentle and cautious fingers. Beneath is a soft and moist coating, just as sadness always nestles under anger. Within that is the sweet fruit.

The waters

At the very heart of the month of willow, we find Valentine's Day, the day of love. Valentine was a Roman saint imprisoned for love and so his devotion is set like a flame upon a backdrop of sacrifice and loss. So it is, that we find this lover's day so placed in the boughs of the grieving tree.

When in therapy we work down through the layers of grief, we always find love to be at the heart of the matter. The love that was lost, the love that never was, the love of self in the face of suffering or the love of what might have been. The love of what is changing, for all things change. We find that grief is a well of ambivalence and ever transmuting feelings. As we near the ache of it, we feel the fear, for as we stare down into the oceanic depths of our heart, we see it magnified as vast as a whale and think, "how can I bear this, how can I birth this, this terrible child of my heart?" So we recoil from grief, and press it down, deeper and harder.

But when grief must come, it will come. Like a baby come to term, it will be born and not all at once but in contractions. Pushing us into rage, then relaxing, pushing us into tears, then relaxing, great cycles of raw and urgent feeling washing over us like waves upon the beach, lasting for what seems like an eternity, until all is spent and peace breaks through the clouds like the first rays of the sunrise.

Whenever we re-enter the womb, in any time of transition, we find her waters rich in grief. Eddies of guilt, swirls of sadness and torrents of anger. The waters of the womb are as diverse and unpredictable as the waters on earth. But just like the terrestrial, they follow a cycle and as we ride upon them, we follow the cycle too.

If we follow the great circle of the waters, we find it begins in the mist upon the sea, drawn up by the sun into the clouds. Then into rain, heavy upon the earth, making puddles and streams. Playful rivulets gather into great curling rivers, sweeping down from the highlands, rushing and pushing. Slow ambient estuaries spread lazily across the flat lands, leading down to the coast. And then the ocean, the great heart, surging, turning and vast. And all along this journey are rapids and whirlpools, lakes and waterfalls, marshes and stagnant ponds. Water with all its many faces, laughing, loving, blustering, relaxing, roaring, thrusting, dozing, round and round and round for ever. So it is with us, if we let it flow, if we become the vessel of our own feeling and not the dam, all passes through us. We tumble down the waterfall into the stillness of a great lake and find rest.

In workshop we can find our place in this great process. We mark out a large circle upon the grass or sand and agree where the sea is (easy if done on a beach). Then feeling into ourselves and reflecting on the last few days, we consider where on the cycle we are at this time. Am I floating in the mist, tumbling with a stream or rolling with the ocean? Am I stuck in a bog or crashing through the rapids? Then we stand on the circle in the appropriate place relative to the sea and checking in with those nearest to us. Using whatever natural materials are to hand we make the image of the state of water that we are feeling upon the ground. Standing behind it we close our eyes and begin to move, staying always fixed to the same point on the ground but letting the water find its natural expression in our body. Slowly we open the flood gates and let

64

the water stretch and twist our bodies into its shapes and patterns, and we open our voices too and let the sounds of the water pour out.

Later, we can move from place to place and using our bodies and our voices, feel our way into the experience of others. When did I last feel like this? These experiences will not be strange to us for the cycle of feeling flows through us all.

A variation on this that goes a little deeper is to draw the feelings onto pieces of slate with white chalk (like moonlit water) and then consider what creature would live beneath its surface. Make an image of this little spirit underneath the slate. Then one by one we can look beneath the surface of our feelings to reveal aspects of ourselves living their secret lives.

In such ways we can begin to see ourselves as part of a never ending flow and cycle, a singing and dancing procession of feeling in which we all take part. This is important for two reasons. Firstly, if we know that feeling moves through us just as water moves through the world then we realize that the way we are feeling today, however terrible, will change. That all we have to do is let go and honour the feeling that is asking to be voiced and then we will move on around the cycle to somewhere else. This knowledge can be life saving.

The second reason is that within relationship feeling tends to polarize towards the most feminine. It then appears to be the sole property of one individual who is perceived as passionate and irrational. In traditional male/female relationships the burden of feeling was often carried by the woman while the man was the builder, organizer and breadwinner. The distance between these poles created a magnetic attraction as each sought wholeness through the other, but it also creates an inevitable lack of understanding, as they are poles apart. Contemporary relationships are less cut and dry but polarizing still occurs. Learning about the cycle of feeling and our part in it helps us to claim back what is ours and release the other from their burden. To carry feeling for yourself and another makes you feel like you are mad. Likewise to carry responsibility and reason for two is a terrible stress. When we take back for ourselves a little of what the other has too much of we make an exchange of the heart. This is the purpose of all relationship.

When grief is born, the waters break. We weep, we cough, we spit and all that was clogged and stuck, a weight upon our heart and our lives, begins to flow. In the space that is left, in that deep well that we feared so much, there comes a great stillness. This is the space in which the seeds of all that we desire can grow. Seeds of joy, love, peace and freedom. Seeds that had no room before. This is the great gift of grief, its rebirthing of our heart.

So Valentine, mysterious symbol of love incarnate, sits in his cell and nurses the flame of love, imprisoned in the place of grief. Waiting for the doors to be unlocked. Waiting for the great release. Waiting to be born again.

The dark mother

Willow speaks to us of the watery womb, the place where the new seeds of our growth are held and sustained, until they are ready to push into consciousness with the coming of the spring. Our relationship with this womb evokes all of our experiences of mothering, both dark and light. Mothering comes in many guises and it not only shapes the people we become, but it teaches us how to mother ourselves as well as others.

Fairytales are particularly rich with archetypal imagery and are not guarded in their portrayal of the dark mother in all her terrifying aspects. For example, in the story of Hansel and Gretel, we meet her twice. First, we meet the cold stepmother who demands that the children be abandoned in the woods, because there is not enough food to go round. This is the starving mother, the one who deprives and neglects, holds back and cannot love. She rejects and abandons the children to save herself. Then we meet the witch, who lives in a house made of candy. She invites the children in to eat what they want, but then she locks up Hansel with the intention of fattening him up for her dinner, whilst making Gretel her slave. She is the candy mother, the one who seduces, promising fulfillment here and now, but then caging and devouring in return. Her candy may be food, sex, alcohol, drugs, gambling or whatever and it holds and satisfies in the moment, but its price is dependency and self-ruin. Often when our experience of mothering is at the hands of the starving mother in whatever form, we wander through the woods, like Hansel and Gretel and are easy prey for she who lives in the candy house. In the end, it is Gretel who, through her own trials, learns what it means to be a good mother, protecting her brother and eventually destroying the witch.

So it is for us, when aspects of our own experience of mothering have been dark, dysfunctional or destructive. If we have been unheld then we will not know how to hold ourselves. If we have been abandoned, then we will expect others to abandon us and we will abandon ourselves as well. If we were not heard, we will not listen to ourselves. If our needs were not honoured, we will probably not honour them now. This is the cold legacy of dark mothering. But like Gretel, through the course of our own trials, we can teach ourselves to mother well.

Willow invites us to honour the dark womb and the light. It invites us to look with courage and honesty at how unconscious parenting or conscious abuse have shaped the course of our lives, and at how we mother others and ourselves in consequence. Often we may 'good mother' our own children in reaction to our own experience of mothering, but we continue the dark legacy in relation to ourselves, sacrificing our own needs, not listening to the child within. How can we make a new womb for that child? How can we cherish, feed, protect and honour the new seeds within ourselves?

The dark mother is a fearful and archetypal presence within and around us. In the forest she is the spirit of destruction and decay that breaks down the old to make room for the new. She can seem cruel and relentless. She is the gale that tears down trees, the predator that raids the nest to devour the chicks, the flood that drowns all in its path. She is the dark face of Nature and she is essential for the balance and maintenance of all things. Yet we fear her and so often deny her a home within ourselves. If we give her no voice or means of expression in our lives then she takes hold of us in other ways and devours us from the inside out. She can make us ill, and if still we do not listen, she can kill us.

The Russian fairytale Vasilisa the beautiful tell us much about her power and its limitations. The child Vasilisa is sent into the forest by her jealous stepmother to beg fire from the witch, the Baba Yaga. The stepmother and her mean spirited daughters hope that the witch will consume her. The Baba Yaga lives in a shack that walks around on chicken legs and even the day and the night are her servants. She would indeed eat the child, should Vasilisa give her cause to, but despite her terrible powers she cannot harm her. This is because Vasilisa carries two totems of her true mother's love. The first is a magic doll that her mother gave her on her deathbed. She has only to feed the doll and it comes to life and completes every task that the witch sets her, however impossible. The doll is a totem of the inner child. So it is with us that if we nourish and listen to the child within we can find guidance and support in the darkest places. The second is her mother's blessing and when we are blessed by the good mother within us we are much less likely to invite harm from the world.

Vasilisa leaves the witch's shack with a flaming skull and when she returns home its blazing eyes set alight and consume the stepmother and stepsisters. To face the dark mother and return with one's own fire of destruction is a vital rite of passage, essential for the attainment of true adulthood. This is why adolescence so often involves a flirtation with this destructive energy. In the absence of organized initiation, antisocial activity and drug culture offers an encounter with the powers of self destruction, lawlessness and chaos that are the attributes of the dark mother. To free ourselves from the mothering of our childhood we must meet and embrace this terrible shadow and return with our own skull full of fire. By depriving our young people of ritual initiation we leave them no choice but to do it themselves, with all the inherent dangers that this implies.

The heart and the moon

All bodies of water including ourselves are tidal and tides are on the moon's puppet strings. So the ebb and flow of our feelings waltz arm in arm with the waxing and waning of the moon. The heart and the moon fill together. When the moon is dark we may feel removed from our feelings, shadowy, confused and head bound, but as she begins to fill, our feelings can become more intense and reach resolution with her fullness. The menstrual cycle is a physical manifestation of this. The cycles of the moon and of the feminine dance together.

Willow was sacred to the moon goddess Hecate, a dark and ancient titan that even Zeus would not challenge. Hecate stands at the crossroads between this world and the underworld and she sees all. She is the dark side of the moon, the deep psychic undercurrents that carry moments of deep knowledge into our dreams and intuitions. She was the goddess of witches and the Greek sorceress Circe had a graveyard of willows dedicated to her on the shore of the river Styx. In the branches of these willows were the bodies of slain warriors, wrapped in ox hide for the birds to devour.

We too must bury our dead if we are to move on. Those we have lost and those aspects of ourselves, our youth, our roles and our relationships that have died. To truly honour and release grief we must separate out its feeling parts from the cauldron that holds the whole. We can make little effigies of those aspects of ourselves that have died, wrap them in leaves, fleece or leather and bind them with willow. Then we can place them in trees like Circe and speak our last words of goodbye.

Hecate is an aspect of the dark mother and here in the womb she will emerge. In leaving the womb we leave mother too and meet her ambivalence just as we meet ours. The cycle of life compels her to expel us, to push us as fledglings out of the nest. Yet still she would contain us, smother us, keep her babies forever. Like Kali she would devour us, reintegrate us into her being. This is the love that squeezes to death. It is also the love that squeezes us out. Sometimes we have to have the last breath crushed out of us before we can surface and breathe for ourselves.

To go willingly into grief, to learn and develop its ways as a practice for life, is a great gift to ourselves and to our children who then learn not to fear it as we did. Once the practice of active grief is learnt, we can feel our way all the way back to our beginnings seeking out the grief that was held there and releasing it now. Tears for the mother that didn't hold us. Anger for the father who frightened us with his rage. Love for the child that we were, so soft, vulnerable and so innocent. Letting go, letting go, letting go. Each time we cut the strings that hold us back and bind us into familiar patterns and self-fulfilling prophecies, we take a leap. We leap into the unknown, into a place where anything is possible and long forbidden dreams can manifest themselves at last.

If we look at a single human life, we can see how cycles of seven years define the stages of development. Infancy, the first seven years, begins with the descent from grace that is our birth and remains a relatively unconscious time within which we develop our creativity, play and emotional world. The second seven make up the childhood we remember, when we are ready to learn the complex codes of letters, numbers and social nuances that allow us to function in the world. Adolescence, with all its torments and wonders, carries us from fourteen to twenty one, the traditional coming of age. The next seven end with Saturn's return, a notoriously challenging transition in our late twenties. Thirty five holds the promise of growth into a fuller experience of adulthood, while forty two marks the point of mid-life crisis. Forty nine invites a maturation into our authority as elder adults while menopause is usually upon us by fifty six. If we examine this we see that every other transition is a dark one within which we are called upon to descend. Adolescence confronts us with the grief of our childhood which must be honoured if we are to become truly adult. Saturn's return invites us to break out from all that confines and entraps us. Mid life compels us to descend into the repressed and shadowy realms of our lives and reclaim all that has been abandoned there. The menopause invites us again into a harsh arena to slay the demons that we must in order to embrace the next stage of life. It would appear that we are meant to spend half of our lives actively engaged in grief. In the story of the two trees in the Garden of Eden we meet the angel with a flaming sword that keeps the way to the Tree of life. So it is that we must be cut down on our journey in order to eat the fruit of this tree. Grief is an essential pre-requisite to life. It deepens us; it brings wisdom and a sense of soul to our lives. It teaches us who we really are and releases us to become just that.

The safe harbour

The expression of love without its shadow is a hollow, artificial thing and although a child will seek it in the absence of real love, in their heart they will rage against it. In their earliest years children begin to explore their capacity for grief. In their tears, terrors and tantrums they taste the fruit of the tree of life. How we respond to this sets the course for the development of their feeling selves. If we stamp on it we squash the feminine into the shadows. If we attempt to distract them we trivialize and dishonour their experience. If we rage back at them we frighten them from feeling. But if we set clear and safe boundaries so that they know where the edge is and then allow and honour their feelings, we give them a great gift. If they find that after the storm, love is a safe harbour waiting to welcome them home, then the world of feeling becomes a safe and familiar one to them. A world in which they can thrive. A world in which they can learn to accept all that they are. A world in which they can learn to love themselves.

If this was not done for us then becoming our own safe harbour can be difficult. To love ourselves can be hard as we often judge ourselves much harsher than we judge others. Sometimes we feel so unlovable and remember only the criticism and condemnation of those that had an investment in making us feel small. It is good to focus on the other side of this. Lie down in a dark place, in a womb, and ask a friend to light a nightlight and place it at your head. This is for the love of yourself. Now one by one name family, lovers, friends (even pets) that have ever loved you. For each name another nightlight must be lit and placed around you. When you can think of no more, sit up and feel the circle of love that has surrounded you all of your life. Even if the lights are few, they will burn all the brighter for that.

We can take photographs or make images of ourselves and place them in a shrine, perhaps in the hollow of a tree or on a rock in the river. Or we can make our heart and sit within it. Gather in this special place tokens of love for yourself. Symbols of what you admire in yourself, promises of self acceptance, trust and loyalty. Commit to treat yourself with the same love that you bestow on others, to give yourself time and opportunity to do the things that make your heart sing. To treat yourself with gentleness and respect. It is traditional when making such promises beneath a weeping willow tree to tie a knot in a length of willow for each promise made so that they are binding. Willow itself is perfect for making such a shrine. Like love it will grow where ever its shoots are planted and it can be woven to make a living womb in which your treasures can be held and the seeds of a new relationship with yourselves can be planted. Then as spring returns to the world the shrine of your heart will burst into life again.

So it is with grief. At first it seems all consuming, like an eternal winter. But as we honour and release it the sunshine begins to return. Although the feelings return in waves again and again they grow less in intensity until one day we find ourselves sitting in the sun and we know in our hearts that the winter is ending. That life is full of hope once more. That spring is round the corner.

Chapter 5   March

The ashes

Fairy tales like Cinderella and Ashlepattle tell us how the feminine emerges from the ashes to blossom and find its own glory. Here at the beginning of March, we find ourselves still sitting in the hearth, waiting for the fire to be lit. Traditionally this is the time when the winter stores would have become depleted, and our patience too. We can feel the promise of spring and we long for its arrival but winter still has her claws in us. In the Christian calendar much of March is given up to Lent. This is a time of contemplation and abstinence in preparation for Easter. It would have marked the time of scarcity before the new food could be gathered. The last of the winter fuel would be used for the fires upon which the last of the winter supplies were cooked to make pancakes, on Shrove Tuesday. Then in the ashes of Ash Wednesday, a time of emptiness and surrender would begin.

The Vikings were called the Aesling or men of ash. The ash tree is the tree that the Celtic people associated most with the month of March. For the Viking, it was Ygdrassil, the World ash. This ancient and shamanic image illustrates three levels of consciousness, as well as the journey of a human life.

The roots of Ygdrassil are found in the underworld, the unconscious self. Because it contains all the material that we have chosen to repress it is also our past and in particular our childhood. It is our foundation, the place that we are growing from. Everything that emerges in our life emerges from here. In the myth of Ygdrassil, the world serpent gnaws incessantly at these roots. Once again the symbol of the dark feminine, the gnawing of the serpent is the gnawing of our wounds demanding attention. This dark material is the compost from which life blossoms. The alchemists call it the prima materia, the dark lead that lies heavy on our hearts. It is the raw product that we must use to make our magic in the world, but it is terrible to us in this state. By the time we emerge from childhood into adolescence it has been laid down inside us. The struggle of adolescence is often a first meeting with this. Prima materia. First matter. First mother. It is the by-product of unconscious parenting, the inevitable wounding of a soft and fragile spirit by forces greater than itself who know no better, or worse, who intend to harm it.

Down among the dark roots of the World ash, we connect very deeply to this child feminine and feel her wounds as raw and intolerable once again. Up among the branches at this time, the buds of the ash tree are black as lead.

We can use ashes in our artwork and our ritual. Lie or sit down somewhere hard and cold and close your eyes. Imagine yourself in a barren and desolate place, a place of ruin and despair. Walk slowly through this no man's land until you come to a pit in the ground. The pit is filled with ashes. As you peer in something moves. There is something alive in there. What is it? Now make an image of this creature using clay or mud, stone or coal and cover it with ash.

Our first glimpse of the prima materia, those twisted and ruined aspects of ourselves, can be harsh and disturbing. But all transformation requires a descent into these ashes and there is no transformation more pressing than spring. There are times in our lives, times of transition, when we will embody the creature in the pit and, to our despair, find ourselves back among the ashes. March teaches us that, terrible as this may seem, it is a vital first stage in a great and mysterious alchemy that, stretching over many years, will transform us into someone else. Someone we have dreamed of but perhaps never dared believe we could become.

Sometimes we make faces, cover them with ash and place them among the roots of trees. Pained and fearful faces, silent screams held bound among the cobwebs, broken spirits, anguish incarnate, yearning, begging, watching, waiting. We can address them, these shades of self; let them feel the touch of fingertips on their cold and ashen faces, even a kiss. In meeting them, in honouring them, we begin to draw the poison like snake venom sucked from the bite. At this time in March they can fill us up, these faces. There is no beginning without them. To the alchemist this is nigredo, the blackening. Here we begin to work the lead that anchors us to the past. Here the alchemy of spring begins.

Sometimes we cover ourselves with ashes and going down to the river, we wash them away.

Releasing the wolf

Just as water is a metaphor for feeling, fire is a metaphor for power and the manner in which it manifests itself, our passion, our authority or our rage. Now that this flame has been lit in the belly of the mother, it begins to grow. In order for spring to come, we now need the masculine principle, the thrust up through the soil, the child to emerge from the womb. Miraculously, it must all happen within this month. At the beginning of March all is slumbering still in the cold embrace of the earth. By the end, spring will have arrived. The power to make this happen must be urgent, unyielding and persuasive. We feel this power arise within ourselves and it can force open the lid of Pandora's box and expose us and others to the shadows within. Often the scariest brute in the box is our anger. In our culture today, it is hard to know where to release this, but this was not always the case.

The Viking tribes that once raided the shores of northern Europe had a living relationship with anger. Their berserker or bear shirt warriors evoked their own rage to such an extent that it produced in them an ecstatic trance. In this state they felt indestructible and felt no pain in battle. This would serve them well as they ran into a storm of swords, axes and arrows. By harnessing their anger, they empowered themselves in the face of great danger. Anger is the knife, the cutting edge of the masculine. The feminine is the sheath, the compassion and sensitivity to others that we need in order to use our knife with integrity. But if we cannot un-sheath it, then we are impotent and powerless.

The ancient Norse story of the three children of Loki has much to teach us about our relationship with anger. Once, when preparing a workshop on this myth, I came across a crescent shaped patch in the long grass. As I took another step, a hare leapt up and away. The patch had been its bed for the night, perhaps this is why hares were sacred to the moon goddess. The hare ran into a natural tunnel in the bushes. I followed it and came out into another part of the field. I decided to use this tunnel in the workshop.

Loki was the trickster god of the Vikings and he carried the shadow for all the great heroes of Asgard. He had three monstrous children. The first was Hel, the guardian of the underworld and in our workshop it was she that we first met when we faced descent. The face of Hel is terrifying because she reflects back to us our own fear. In the workshop the group was split into two and each group used their bodies and voices to make the face of Hel. The other group would meet this face and as honestly as possible confess their fears about confronting their own anger. Only then, when all had shared, could they pass through the hare's tunnel into the underworld.

Loki's second child was Fenrir the great wolf. Fenrir was so fierce that the gods ordered him chained but no bonds were strong enough to contain him. So the gods asked the dwarves to fashion chains that Fenrir could not break. This they did, making them from intangible things like the root of a mountain and the sound a cat makes when it stretches. These were placed upon Fenrir and the god Balder placed his right hand in the wolf's mouth as a sign of trust. The more the wolf struggled the tighter the chains became, biting into his flesh, until at last he was subdued. Balder lost his hand.

We too bind our anger with intangible things: guilt, shame, reason, addiction and fear. We too sacrifice our right hand, our God given power, when we do so. In the workshop we took turns to be the wolf, bound by all the hands that could hold us. We raged against these unbreakable chains. We raged until we were exhausted. Then having felt the force that we keep reined up inside us we made effigies of those aspects of self or others that we would unleash this force upon. Using our words of power, our voices and our bodies, we released the wolf and destroyed the effigies.

The group formed a holding circle around each of us as we raged. This therapeutic space, this sealed container, allows the fire to burn safely, to have its time and its place. It also represented the third of Loki's children, the Midgard serpent that coils around the world. Once again a symbol of the dark feminine, the serpent is the wound that underlies all. It is this wound that the anger protects like a dog. When the anger is released it is this wound that we feel beneath. As each of us released our rage, the sadness held below rose to the surface and the holding group closed in to hold the soft and fragile soul within.

The sealed container

In the Greek myth of Persephone, we meet once again the feminine imprisoned in the underworld. Captured by the dark God Hades she is held beneath the earth and her mother Demeter, who clothes the Earth in green, mourns the loss of her daughter, bringing the first winter to the world. In the end it is the intervention of Zeus, the thunder god, which secures Persephone's release, albeit only for half the year. For

75

Persephone must return again to the underworld each autumn. And so every spring Demeter celebrates the return of her daughter Persephone by returning life to the land.

We too need a little of our own thunder to rise up out of the ashes. The prima materia we find there, the wounded child nursing its pain, is almost unbearable to us in this raw and original state. Although we connect once again to this child we are no longer children and we can react as adults to its suffering. It is this reaction, the fire of our anger, which begins the alchemy. It is the heating of the sealed container, the buried seed, the alchemical retort within which the magic unfolds. It is the fight in us that cries "I will not be back in this place again!" It is the desperate push of the seedling up and out of the dirt. It is spring.

The word spring evokes the image of feeling pushing up and bursting out of the darkness as in a spring of water. There is a point usually around mid March when we can feel this happen, both in ourselves and in the land. On our journey up the World ash this is when we meet the surface and find the light. There we can breathe a sigh of relief as we feel that we are at last out of the ashes.

We can also meet great resistance here, especially if we struggle to contain our fire and do not let its power push us up through the cold crust of the earth. Both the mythic heroes Odin and Achilles had spears made of ash and we too may need to direct our anger, spear-like, to pierce the cold shroud that contains us and feel the warmth of the sun again. To fight back against the ashes that would smother us. To break the waters and birth ourselves.

Making and using our own spear allows us to ritualize this. Young ash grows slender but strong and makes a fine shaft. We tip them with slate or flint, shards of bone or shell, and bind them with strips of leather or sheep's wool. Then we decorate them lightly to make them our own but not interfere with their flight. Sometimes we make images on the ground out of ashes to represent the old self, that which seeks to contain and restrict us. Then, shouting our words of power, we hurl our spears to pierce these ashes, opening the surface of the earth so that the child can emerge once again.

We can turn our anger too on the rubbish that we find in Nature. Litter and abandoned objects reflect the poisons within ourselves, other people's shadows dumped on us. We can make art with this dark material, release our rage upon it, and then burn it or take it home with us and dispose of it properly. So the feminine is cleansed and renewed by fire. On the body of the ash tree grows a fungus commonly known as King Alfred's cakes. This lead black substance will hold and nurture a spark if one is placed upon it and so it is often used in fire making. So it is that ash welcomes and feeds our fire.

All initiation draws upon this process. The ritual itself is the sealed container, within which the initiate can experience nigredo and then fight their way up and out of the ashes to emerge reborn into a new level of adulthood. When we do not initiate our young, they will seek the process themselves among their peers but without initiating elder or container, this is dangerous. Many of us, adults and parents at this time, were not initiated and so do not know how to give this precious gift to our children. As long as the child within us is still waiting for the initiating elder who never comes we will be unable to step into those footsteps and become that elder for our young. Yet we can embrace initiation at any age, however belated.

If we cannot find the elders to initiate us, then we must turn to the wisest elder of all, Nature.

Time alone in Nature is a great leveler. The more simply we live, the more we learn about ourselves. Meeting the real challengers of hunger, cold, wet, insects, getting lost, long dark nights and being alone with ourselves and our feelings forces us down into our ashes and deepens and strengthens our relationship with self. Paths unveil themselves to us, drawing us into mysterious and mythic encounters with aspects of self reflected among the shadows of the forest. Here, a deer slips almost unseen into the darkness. Follow me, it says. There, a great wounded oak nurses its lightning struck heart, a secret cave within its body. Climb inside, it says. Here, the stream leads us down to a natural pool carved among the rocks, a dark and shadowy cauldron filled with ice cold water. Bathe in me, it says. There, the great ash tree pushes up into the canopy above to kiss the sun. Climb me, it says. Nature serves up our fears one by one and as we face and overcome them we change. As we open to her wisdom we learn how she guides and protects us. Fear is replaced by trust. The spirits of the wild stand around us like a circle of elders and honour us as one of them. When we come home, we are not the same.

Ygdrassil had a spring at its roots known as the Well of Urd. Here dwelt three wise women, the Norns, who oversaw the destinies of men and their names were Fate, Being and Necessity. They were associated with childbirth and they stand awaiting our rebirth from the roots each spring. To the Celts, the ash was also associated with rebirth and new life. In this context ash was used to heal sick children, who were passed through a split in the trunk. The trunk was then bound and prayed over. If the tree healed, it was believed the child would also be healed.

We too must pass through the alchemy of ash to heal the child within. We cannot change our roots, they are all that we have to grow from, but we can transform the child's pain into the adult's power. This is why so many healers end up working in the area that mirrors their own wounding.

Ash invites us to fight our way out of the ashes so that the child self can feel the sun again. In every rebirth, it is the child that first emerges, the soft and urgent seedling. To reclaim the qualities of the child: their play, their trust, their spontaneity, their openness, their wonder, their joy of life, is our challenge as adults. Here, as spring begins, when the birds start making their nests and the lambs play in the field, the spirit of the child is everywhere.

Emerging

Miracle of miracles. Everywhere we look little green fists push up and out of the soil and open their hands to touch the sun. Down in the dark dens the sleepers stretch and yawn. Life begins to creep, and hop and scurry once again. Colour returns. The daffodils, golden cups of sunshine held aloft for all to drink from. The mosses, vibrant green carpets that tempt us down onto the earth. The first scattering of blossom, like soft new snow among the hedgerows. Cinderella has risen from the ashes, and putting on her new dress, she dances with her solar prince.

The trunk of Ygdrassil is the here and now, this world that we live in, the present. It is here that the alchemical transformation of the prima materia takes place. When we allow ourselves to be in relationship with our feminine, to be present in the here and now and feel, we begin the transmutation of our wounds, changing the lead into gold. This is conscious adulthood, our life work. In the myth of Ygdrassil, there is a squirrel scurrying up and down between the roots and the branches. Such is human nature, scurrying up and down between heaven and hell, dwelling on the past, planning for the future. We need to still the squirrel in order to be present, only then can we really feel. Then the trunk of the tree again becomes the sealed container in which the process unfolds as naturally as the spring.

Learning to be, becoming mindful of the here and now, can help the child to emerge. The mind has a thousand distractions with which it can keep us from feeling. Jobs to do, plans to make, mistakes to mull over, worries to dwell upon, addictions to satisfy. We may say "when I've done this, I'll have some time for myself." But it never comes because there is always more to do. The only time to stop is right now.

When we still ourselves we begin to hear the child feminine whispering up from the roots. She is naturally wild. She cries when she is sad, rages when she is angry and seeks comfort when she is scared. When she is happy she is the very personification of joy and she loves with a fiery passion. All she desires is to love and be loved and to be allowed to be. But family and society often persuade us to keep our feelings to ourselves and by the time we are adults we may have replaced her with a stiff upper lip, a tied tongue and a well defended heart. But that is not her nature. Her nature is to run like the wolf and roar like the lion. Or just to be, like the lilies in the field.

Lie on the forest floor looking up at the trees. See how the canopy of branches above float like islands in an ocean of blue. See how they make maps upon the sky. Look for your journey there. Allow yourself to settle into stillness. Allow yourself to be. Allow time to pass. Imagine the roots below you. What is emerging in you now, bubbling up from the roots of your being like a sacred spring? Let it rise and if it has a voice, let it come. Sing it up into the treetops, let it play, let it flower, let it fly.

I remember once arriving at the door of a creative therapy centre and seeing in front of the step a seedling emerging. This fragile little spirit, so soft that I could have crushed it between my finger and thumb, had pushed its way up through tarmac, creating a little crater out of which it was arising. It seemed to me the perfect symbol for creative therapy. This is the power of the spring, the power we can harness within ourselves to push up through whatever would smother and oppress us.

This is a good time to plant seeds and we can do so in ritual, affirming what it is that we are sowing in ourselves, or to create images as they grow. On a road verge near my home someone planted the word "peace" in daffodil bulbs. Every spring peace would come to us as we drove by, in bright golden letters. Working with images on the ground can be useful too. Often we use materials that birds and wildlife can eat for the creatures are experiencing their own Lent as they wait for spring to feed them again. Some of these images can be vast. Using flour to make white lines upon the ground we can draw great and mythic symbols upon our hillsides, images of the newly awakened creatures that we have encountered or of the spirits emerging within ourselves.

This is the time to play too, for in playing we release the child back into the world. Chasing, climbing, wrestling, rolling down hills, damming streams, building dens, making up stories, sharing adventures, why should these pleasures be reserved for children alone? They liberate us from our roles and routines, they thrill and empower us, they rekindle relationship with our bodies, with the earth and with each other. They bring us joy, that most elusive of adult emotions. In our fantasies we inhabit a world of metaphor, as do children in their play. We rediscover our pathways through its mysterious terrain. We relearn its secret language. This is essential because metaphor is the hermetic link between the inner and outer worlds. Without it we cannot find or release the feminine. Just as stone is the foundation of the material world, metaphor is the foundation of the metaphysical. So metaphor is truly the philosopher's stone, and only metaphor can turn lead into gold.

Climbing the tree

As spring awakens around us, we reach the equinox on the 21st March. This is a point of balance as the length of the days and nights become equal. This is half-way up the World ash, a point of equilibrium between the dark lead among the roots and the gold within the branches, between the lunar feminine and the solar masculine. This can be a turning point, as we reconcile an aspect of the inner child's wounding and find strength and peace once again. The sun is shining. The colours are awakening. This is a place of hope.

We have often dressed the trunks of trees at this time, showing what is flowering for us or honouring the death of old ways. We can use thorns to pin soft materials such as leaves, flowers, fleece and feathers to bark and we can use this to show our journey up from the roots. Harder thing such as bones, shells, seeds and stones can be pushed into cracks and crevices in the body of the tree. It is like decorating ourselves. Like a child at the Christmas tree we see ourselves reflected in its treasures.

As we climb higher through the month, we begin to feel the changes unfolding within us. Here in the Christian calendar begins the countdown to Easter. Symbolically, Christ was nailed high upon this tree. This is the death of the old self, just at the point of rebirth, and we can feel this here and the anxiety and grief that it brings. But it is essential, for crucifixion is the pathway to ascension, the means by which we transmute the poisons of our past into the formulas that will empower and release us. Just as the dragonfly larvae, suspended with its kin beneath the dark surface of the pond, appears to shrivel and die at the moment that the dragon-fly emerges above into a world a thousand times more expansive, with wings.

We can feel the resistance to this death as winter struggles to retain us in the face of spring. In the story of Rapunzel the feminine is imprisoned in a tower, looking out at the world and longing. So it can seem for us, here in the trunk of the World ash, cocooned and transmutating into something unknown. Rapunzel waits in a place of transition between winter, the old witch, and spring, the young prince. Winter seeks to keep us imprisoned. Spring desires our freedom.

In the branches of Ygdrassil, we find the future and those elders who having worked their alchemy are now harvesting their gold. In the myth, the lower branches are the home of deer, which graze upon the leaves. As symbols of love and gentleness, the deer are an indication of the nature of this harvest. We may strive for material wealth but it is in the fruiting of relationship, both with ourselves and others, that we find real gold. This is a harvest of the heart and it can be there in all our futures. We can make treasures and hang them among the branches to honour this. Beautiful clusters of crystal, hazel catkins, spring flowers, soft worn glass from the beach, little clay birds dressed in real feathers, fools gold and precious stones suspended like fruit alongside fat balls rolled in seed for the birds to enjoy. Or we can climb a tree and sit there, contemplating the riches around us. There is so much gold about at this time as the pussy willows flower, gorse petals emblazon the cliff tops and moor land and daffodils and primroses carpet the woodland.

The arrival of the deer in the unfolding of the myth marks the return of warmth to the world. As together we all emerge from the ashes, we find a spring in our step and a little more sunshine in our dealings with each other. There can be great playfulness here, as the child shakes off its chains and learns to dance again. The keys to these chains are there too if we look, for the seeds of the ash tree are called ash keys and bunches of last year's will still be suspended among the branches of some trees. Sometimes at this time we make the chains that bind us and unlock them with an ash key. They are the seeds to all that we would be should the child within us be untethered and allowed to blossom and grow. It is said that ash keys unlock magic doors in the tree's trunk so for us they unlock our understanding of the process that has unfolded within us. As we look down from the branches we can honour the journey that we have made from the unconscious and fearful world of the child to the consciousness and courage of adulthood. We can begin to see the treasure that we harvest from the ashes of the past. It was here, hanging among the keys of the ash, that Odin finally understood the meaning of the runes. This is the wisdom that only feeling can bring. Only when we feel our truth, do we know it to be true.

Once some friends and I found a pile of stones surrounded by a circle of ash trees. We built the stones into a throne, made a crown of ash and crowned each other. Prior to each coronation we shared three things that we had collected to represent body, mind and spirit. I had found an empty old tin cup for body and wandered down to the river to fill it with water, to symbolize feeling. I bent down and scooped up some water, only to find a single ash key floating in my cup, rescued from the river against all odds. This is the way of therapeutic synchronicity, a message from the higher self connected to all things that tells us that we are on the right path. This is the mystery unlocked by the Ash key, the alchemy of matter becoming spirit and spirit becoming matter.

The coronation that occurs at the head of the tree marks our becoming the rulers of our own kingdoms, ourselves. As we learn to release the fettered feelings of the wounded child within we cease to be at the mercy of their unconscious reactions, triggered by the people in our lives who remind us of oppressors or abusers we have known. Now we can begin to live consciously.

The World ash is the centre pole of the universe; it connects the microcosm to the macrocosm. So the myth can be read at many levels. It is the story of spring. It is the journey of a human life. It is the cycle of the year that begins in descent and arises through empowerment into freedom. Perhaps most potent of all, it is a magical recipe for the transformation of all struggle into glory. On a daily basis we can use this to transcend anything that stands in our way. Everything that emerges in our life, including the obstacles that manifest themselves before us, emerges from the roots, the domain of the wounded child. So whenever we find ourselves stuck, troubled, oppressed, frustrated, overwhelmed or defeated, this is where we must go. Back into the ashes to seek the child. Using the language of metaphor we find and release the feeling hidden there. We shout, we weep, we recover. Things change. We have learned the lesson that was waiting for us, so the problem fades away. This is real magic.

But this is not just a recipe for dealing with emotional issues, major traumas or relationship problems, even the most practical and mundane of dilemmas can be resolved in this way. For example I began driving very late in life. My first mock driving test was a disaster. I almost caused an accident and the instructor, shocked at how little I looked in the mirror, told me that I was months away from passing. I thought about the mirror. I remembered as a child looking into that mirror from the back seat and seeing my father's face. I realized I was scared of seeing that face again, of becoming my father, whose manhood was defined by the long hours that he worked away from home and by his role as the driver. My father was dead, but I went out into Nature and talked to him anyway. I got angry and I cried. Then, just two weeks after the mock exam, I passed my driving test.

The more we practice this alchemy the more natural it becomes and the quicker we can process our experiences and consciously manifest change. Metaphor becomes our second language. We find ourselves functioning on a higher, more conscious, plane. Walking, as it were, with the angels.

At the top of the tree sits the eagle, the higher self. Looking upon our whole life, we can understand the meaning of our journey, no longer caught up in its illusions. Now we can see the wood for the trees. So then the work is done. We take our final breath and the eagle spreads its wings and leaves the body.

Odin hung himself upon this tree. Buddha sat beneath it. Christ was nailed to it. All surrendered themselves to the feminine. They received, felt and suffered their wounds. The mysteries were revealed to them and they soared like eagles.

This overview is in the eye of the eagle that sits upon Ygdrassil like the phoenix arisen from the ashes. Here the ash flowers, the black buds bursting open into purple florets, the colour of royalty. Here is the throne, where Cinderella is crowned and seated, the child transformed, her ashes turned into golden robes. For here in this World ash, so steeped in the masculine, in fire and force and Viking gods, the feminine has risen like sap and blossomed. In and around the fields the mad march hares, origin of our Easter bunny, dance in dedication to the moon goddess to whom they are sacred. Spring is here. The world is reborn.

Yet in the story of Rapunzel the prince does not carry off his princess straight away. When he climbs the tower to rescue her he finds her gone and instead the witch awaits him. She casts him from the tower into the thorns below. We too ascend the tree in search of the newly crowned feminine, the virgin spring. We too find the thorns awaiting us.

Chapter 6   April

The thorns

Sunshine. How it tantalizes and seduces us. Come, it says, cast open the doors to your heart and let me in. Shake off your shaggy winter coats and come play in my garden. The sunshine of April is like first love. It makes fools of us.

The month of April begins with April fool's day. In the tarot, the fool is the first card, the unnumbered card, and represents the child in all its innocence. We see the fool chasing a butterfly and stepping off a cliff. It is an image of absolute trust.

So it is that having climbed the ash tree and reclaimed the child within, we are seduced by the butterfly of spring, its sunshine and its promise. We step off the edge, just to tumble back into feeling.

Can we ever forget that first fall from first love? How harsh were those thorns? How they tear and rend the child's heart within us. But how vital and unavoidable these black and bitter thorns, so that when true love comes, we can know its shadow and step through its doorway as lovers not fools.

The tree that the Celts traditionally associated with April was the hawthorn, a tree of love and fertility. But the hawthorn does not usually flower until May which is why it is also called the May tree. The blackthorn flowers now, around Easter. Its soft white blossom is in stark contrast to its harsh black thorns. Known as the crown of thorns, the blackthorn tells us of the difficult tasks that must be faced, indeed, that cannot be avoided. This is the place of shadow that must be honoured before the fullness of spring can be enjoyed.

When the Christian church arrived in these Celtic lands, it aligned the story of the crucifixion and resurrection of Christ with the pagan festival of Eostre, goddess of spring. In doing so it recognized and honoured this path through the shadow of black thorn. The symbol of Eostre is the egg and she rests at the root of the words oestrus and oestrogen. She is the original reason we give Easter eggs.

The crucifixion is an archetypal and alchemical image of the transformation of suffering into glory. Nailed to wood, unable to do anything, only to receive and to feel. Fixed to the feminine, as one with the tree. This image invites us to go willingly into the place of greatest resistance, the place of our own suffering, to be our own suffering, to surrender intent and hope and to let our grief flow through us like blood. Only then can we ascend, be released and transformed.

But between the cross and glory there is a transitional time, the time spent lying in the tomb, a time of waiting, pupating, like the caterpillar in its chrysalis. Like the chick in the egg.

So spring is here and we can feel its cardinal and vibrant energy growing inside us. The desire to emerge into new life, pursue new goals and seek out new paths can be strong within us, yet somehow the time is not yet right. The days can still be cool and wet, the nights cold, and like the chick in the egg there is a sense that we are born but not yet hatched. There is a tension here, an expectation that cannot yet be fulfilled. The chick in the egg is not alone, he has his yolk sac, a vestige of the womb, the old self. Before he can hatch he must consume and digest this dark twin. This is the aspect of self that must die for the chick to live.

Blackthorns are long and sharp like needles. We can use them to pin things together or onto trees. We can make totems of the old self or of the difficult tasks that must be undertaken before we can run free. We can take these with us into quiet dens made in the woods. Waiting, in stillness, in silence, we begin to digest the shadow. Shadow is the suns dark twin and one cannot exist without the other. So with the sun's return comes shadow too. We must know the sun's shadow in order to become its lover. We must know our own shadow in order to love. As a group we can spend hours in these silent tombs, until someone comes to roll back the stone. We can ask for the nature of our awakening. Perhaps a song. Perhaps a garland of spring flowers. Perhaps a rain of soft white blackthorn blossom falling like confetti upon our new selves. Perhaps, even, a kiss.

The white track

In the mythology of hawthorn, we hear more of the difficult tasks that must be faced. The hawthorn goddess Olwen was the daughter of

86

Yspaddaden Pencawr or Giant Hawthorn. She was known as 'She of the white track', for white blossom sprang up wherever she walked, leaving white tracks across the land, just as the flowering of hawthorn in the hedgerows does now. The nephew of King Arthur, Culhwych, fell in love with her and was set by her father countless impossible tasks before he could claim her hand. He was helped by the Knights of the Round Table and won his bride.

So Olwen's white track becomes the bridal train leading us across the land to the place of union. Here where the sun and earth are joined in the marriage that is spring, where the masculine and feminine within us become one, this is our inner alchemical wedding. April is the time of preparation for this, where the sacred tasks are set, a time of cleansing, chastity and contemplation.

But just as the hawthorn does not blossom until the end of April, it can be hard in the early part of the month to discern our white track from all the others available to us. Its whiteness, as it were, is not apparent yet. The white track is not a road of oughts and shoulds, it is a path of heart. We may not recognize it until we feel it. Stepping onto it thrills us to the core.

We often spend a lot of April making these white tracks, defining slowly our path of heart upon the land. A furrow weaves across a beach, filled with flour and leads to a shrine among the rocks decorated with crab shell, cuttlefish, and gull feathers. Soft white down, pinned to the body of a tree with thorns, winds its way up into the branches to reach a little bird's nest, reclaimed from the forest floor and made whole and soft again with moss and spring flowers. A spiral of blackthorn blossom unfurls down among the new ferns, leading ever inwards to its heart, a bowl of clay lined with a mosaic of eggshell, into which is poured spring water with which to wash.

As lovers we may walk many tracks before we find the one that shines. As lovers we may face impossible tasks and, like Culhwych, need to call upon all our resources to complete them. As lovers we may often end up back in the thorns. But when the time is right, the tasks completed and the lessons learned, the thorns can part by themselves, just as they do in Sleeping Beauty when the hundred years has passed and the true prince arrives. Then the white track begins to shine.

The white track may lead us to another but it shines because in doing so it leads us to ourselves. A marriage of souls is a mutual quest for inner freedom. When my wife and I were married these were our vows:

Through this wedding I set you free
Follow your dreams and you will find me there

In the face of spells I will always be your ally
I promise you my valiant love in all things
Speaking my heart's truth, seeing every struggle through to its end
So that my love is always your safe harbour
When the storm is spent

I promise never to lessen or sacrifice myself for you
But always to be loyal to my own spirit's needs
So that I can grow stronger in loving you
Laugh and play and thrive with you
Create with you
Be true to you
Cherish and support you in all love's wise and gentle ways

When you are strong I will honour you
When you are small I will nurture you
When you are sad I will hold you
When you are raging I will meet you
 When you are frightened I will be your rock
When you are soaring I will dance like the wind beside you

I promise to make time for us
For the light and the shadow of us
Time to seek and find our hearts again
Time to languish in our love and begin anew

I choose to grow old with you

Ever more expansive

Ever more alive

Ever more in love

Until death places one in the heart of the other

And only love remains

All love is a quest for inner union. All relationship is an exchange in which something of me is given to you and vice versa. But just as it was Olwen's giant father that set the impossible tasks for Culhwych, so it is our parents or parental figures that stand in our way now. All those unresolved feelings from childhood, the anger the child could not express, the sorrow that still awaits its tears, the fear of intimacy that makes us hold back, all carried forward into every new relationship until we find one strong enough to contain them. Then at last we can move beyond them and truly love another, because only when we have honoured and released them can we truly love ourselves.

So when we rage at our loved one, we must ask ourselves, who am I really raging at here? What is he doing that reminds me of my father? In what way is she being like my mother? It may not be obvious at first so look for the metaphor. How does it make you feel? He may not hit you like your father did but his cold disinterest is giving your heart the same message, that you are not worth cherishing. She may not lock you in your bedroom the way your mother did, but her way of always putting the children's needs first still leaves you feeling neglected. Relationship will bring us home to the original wound time and time again until we do something about it.

It is at these times that we might consider abandoning the relationship altogether and finding another instead, because as our partner takes on the mantle of our parent the role of lover falls vacant and someone else may suddenly begin to shine in our eyes. It is important that we recognize this as a spell because if we simply leave one for the other nothing is changed or resolved within ourselves and not only will we have added much heartache, resentment and guilt to our world but we will soon revisit this place again in the new relationship. The other shines because they are embodying the part of our self that is most in need of attention. At these times it might be better to close our senses to the shining one or if this is not possible, tie ourselves to the mast of our determination like

Odysseus so that we can hear the song of the siren but not jump overboard. The work to be done is usually not with the other out there, however inviting this may seem, but with the aching self within.

Once we recognize this a new opportunity presents itself to us. Instead of fight or flight, we have a third option, alliance. Allies face things together, however painful. Allies may not always be friends, but they are always committed to their alliance. The alliance becomes a third body in the partnership and its needs are made paramount. So right at this moment I may hate you, but I am going to work with you any way to find out why, for the sake of our alliance. An alliance has unbreakable rules. Do not hit me. Do not walk out until we have resolved something. Take responsibility for yourself. Commit to look within instead of just blaming me.

Now we can use the other consciously to release feelings that have been bottled up in us for years. The other can represent the parent without taking it personally. They can hold the space and push the buttons. We can rage. We can cry. This time the child is not alone. For when the transference is done and the spell broken our loyal and patient lover waits to hold us.

Of course the white track does not always lead us into relationship with another. Sometimes it leads us out. But it always leads us closer to ourselves.

The bad advisor

As a time of nesting, April holds the egg at its heart. Our desire to break out and ascend to a new cycle of growth is strong but there are other voices too. Just as in the Easter story, crucifixion precedes ascension, so aspects of the old self have to die first.

In the Hebrew story of Esther we meet these conflicting voices. A young Jewish girl is chosen by the king to become his new queen. Her father Mordecai warns her to keep her origins secret, and he waits everyday by the palace gates to hear news of his daughter. There he overhears a plot against the king and sends news of this to Esther. Esther tells the king and the men are hanged. This is recorded in the King's book of chronicles but the king is unaware of Mordecai's part in it.

Unnerved by the plot, the king appoints a new advisor to ensure his safety. This advisor, Haman, is a proud and arrogant man, made all the more so by the appointment. He fears the presence of the Jewish people in the kingdom and fuelling the king's fears he advises him to have them all killed. The king is persuaded and agrees on a date for this to happen. Mordecai hears of this and gets another message to his daughter. Esther must act quickly if her people are to be saved but she dare not approach the King without being summoned, on penalty of death. So she makes herself beautiful to him and when he sees her, love melts his heart. He promises to grant her whatever she desires and she asks that the king and his advisor dine with her on the following day when she will make her petition. That night the king cannot sleep and he asks for the book of chronicles to be read to him. Here he learns about Mordecai's part in revealing the plot against him and that nothing has been done to reward him.

In the meantime Haman, irritated by the old man who hangs around the palace doors and refuses to bow to him, orders a scaffold to be built, upon which he intends to hang Mordecai.

The next day, at dinner with Esther and Haman, the king asks his advisor what should be done to honour a man who has served him above all. In his arrogance Haman assumes that he is talking about him so he advises that such a man should be brought through the city on a white horse, showered with gifts and seated at the king's right side. To his horror he then learns that this man is Mordecai. Then the king asks Esther what it is that she desires. She tells the king that she, his beloved queen, her father Mordecai who had saved his life, and all their people, are doomed. Her petition is that they be saved. The king asks who it is that so threatens them, so that he might strike him down. Esther denounces Haman. The king realizes his mistake and the bad advisor is hung from his own gallows. Then Mordecai is brought into the city on a white horse, showered with gifts and seated at the King's right side as his new advisor.

The king is the primary self. Initially, he is guided by Haman the bad advisor. His voice is loud in the king's ear. His is the voice of fear, the self protective mind, the weak masculine. At this time it may be saying to us 'take no risks; give up on your dreams; play it safe; it is not practical; it will never happen; destroy it all'. Motivated by fear, this voice cannot see beyond the confines of the egg and struggles for power within it. It seeks to keep us confined and under its will, killing anything that threatens it or seeks to be free. It will find others too, people on the outside, who echo its opinions back to us, reinforcing its strength. It is easy to be overwhelmed by and submit to such a voice.

The quiet voice of Esther, the young queen, was less available to the king. So it is that the soft voice of the heart, the feminine, is so easy to ignore unless we seek it. Esther made herself so lovely in his eyes that he stopped and heard her voice. The people were saved. The good father Mordecai, the wise and benevolent masculine who had the higher vision and who had guided her from afar all along, became the new advisor to the king.

Our task here is not just to hear the quiet voice of the feminine but also to unseat the bad advisor and reclaim a healthy masculine. The bad advisor may be a parental figure that we have integrated or a construct that has been evoked in consequence of past traumas. It is protective but cannot see the higher vision and so it keeps us from our dreams. It is this very human body that must be hung on the cross of its own making so that we can ascend to the next cycle of our growth.

But where is the masculine that would replace it? Often this is hidden within us. A fear of our own power or a fear of repeating parental patterns may have sentenced this, our true masculine, to banishment or imprisonment within. Like Mordecai, it waits at the palace gates for news of its beloved, getting messages of wise guidance to her whenever it can.

So we must summon the healthy masculine, the soft and strong within us that seeks only to cherish and protect our feeling selves. We need his power, indeed his righteous anger, to silence the voice of the bad advisor so that we can step forward with courage and faith into our dreams. When he comes, like Mordecai arriving on horseback, he comes riding upon his power like a wave. For when the egg has sat for long enough it is the chick that must crack its way out. This is the new masculine, the active principle that rebels against the fears and doubts that would confine us and shatters the illusion of restriction. We need him because in the inner wedding of spring that is Beltane, he is the true groom. His are the wings upon our shoulders yet to unfold.

Often at this time we make images of the bad advisor within and seat them in a place of power. We write down the bad advice that they are giving us, the words of fear, self doubt and negativity that keep us frozen and disempowered. Reading these words to the group, we stand and face the bad advisor while the others echo the words back to us. We listen, standing them for as long as we can, letting our anger rise. Then using the power in our voice we silence them. " Enough!" "Stop!" "Silence!" We unseat the bad advisor, take our place in the seat of power and speak our higher truth.

Silencing the voice of fear and negativity is a rallying victory in the cause of the higher self and to do so we need muster some real power. Raising the voice is essential for this as the demand for silence must be non negotiable. There are many ways in Nature to practice this. Stand at the foot of a tall tree within which crows are nesting and endeavor to frighten the crows from their nests. Watch how they scatter, then wheel around and return, so that you can practice again. Stand on one side of a valley and try to attract the attention of a person or an animal that you can see on the other. If your voice carries, the horse or cow may lift its head, the farmer turn to listen. Stand on a cliff and roar at the sea, making yourself heard above the waves by another who stands on the beach below. Stand on a mountain and summon your echo. Only when your voice is full of power will the mountains give it back to you.

There are two Tors that I sometimes work on that are within sight of each other and share a legend between them. The story says that King Arthur stood on one and the devil on another, and that they threw rocks at each other. King Arthur won and forced the devil back into Hell. The devil's rocks are those words of negativity that are hurled at us, both by others and by ourselves. They seek to crush and bury us. In the group we share these words with one another and once again the others bombard us with them until we raise our power and shout them down. King Arthur's rocks are the words of truth that honour and empower us. These we shout from the top of the Tor as we stand with arms outstretched in the wild and blustering wind.

Cleansing

As April showers wash away the last vestiges of the old cycle so we are compelled to spring clean our homes in preparation for the new. This is a time of ritual cleansing and we ourselves can feel renewed by this. Entering the water is one of the most immediate ways to make oneself present, to silence the chattering mind and come home to our bodies. Kneeling beside the moorland stream we wash our hands, our hair, our face. Then, from the mud on the bank we mould a little homunculus, a dark little figure to hold all that we would wash away, and give it to the stream. Working on the seashore, we cover each other with sand and seaweed, then rising; we shed these old skins and walk into the sea. Later, when we are gone, the tide comes in to gather up our old and tired selves, shake them out and reuse them for something else. Standing at the foot of a waterfall where, legend has it, the knights of the round table were once baptized, we step into the rush and thunder and surrender ourselves to its great cold hands, pushing us under like a child at the font. Spluttering and shivering we emerge afresh, reborn, recommitted to our quest.

Hawthorn has long been associated with wells and springs. Many of these ancient and wizened trees are seen as guardians of these often sacred places. Here, people would gather to pray and make wishes, to draw water and ritually cleanse, washing away the old to make way for the new. The hawthorns would stand like wise women resplendent in their white robes and oversee all. Young girls on seeing the first blossom of hawthorn would partly break it from the branch and leave it hanging. Then that night, they would dream of their husband to come. If the next day they found and gathered up the broken blossom it was kept as a charm until he arrived. The blossom can be eaten too, as can the leaves, to nourish and open the heart, to infuse with the magic of May. The dew upon the blossom is said to cleanse and purify the skin.

Known as the 'bread and cheese' tree, Hawthorn's leaves and berries are nourishing and have sustained many travelers. Hawthorn sustains us now as we gather our strength and seek out our white track. Hawthorn works also as a heart stimulant, bringing health and vitality to the heart and regulating blood pressure. Hawthorn nourishes and opens our heart to welcome love and fertility, cleansing the way for the wedding to come. It is to the heart that we must attend and listen, if we are to recognize our white track among all the many possible paths that lie before us.

Imagine how the heart cleanses and renews the body. Its rivers of blood flood perpetually through our cells, washing away the toxins and feeding the new life. Once in hospital I was given the chance to see my heart in echoes passed through my chest like the language of bats. The heart is not a still place. The torrent of blood rushed through like red and blue flames. The valves opened and closed like the waving arms of a dancing figure. For me it was an image of Shiva, dancing his never ending cycle of death and rebirth in a circle of fire. Love is like this. It turns upon itself like the great ocean, never still, an eternal celebration of life and death, of joy and sorrow. Sometimes it sweeps us away to another land, another adventure. Sometimes it moves on without us, beyond our reach, leaving us shipwrecked and alone. Sometimes we drown. Sometimes we are borne aloft, sparkling and beautiful like Aphrodite in her shell. As long as the heart beats there is always the chance of renewal. As long as the heart beats, there is always the promise of love.

Just as the heart cleanses the body, so love can cleanse and revive the feeling self. Falling in love is like leaping into a moorland pool. Nothing wakes us up to life like love, it shocks and thrills us to the core, it makes us holler and roar like wild beasts. Love sweeps away the old loyalties to which we cling. Love cauterizes the old wounds from which we recoil. Love can start our life afresh, like a glorious fiery sunrise.

But the foolishness of love comes from the belief that this is all there is. That beyond the initial blaze and bluster, there is only harmony and joy. Each new beginning is a reworking of the old. Love cleanses the space within which this dance must take place again, a slow and painful revisiting of old steps and a mastering of the new. Shiva's dance of destruction and renewal in the fires of the heart.

The impossible tasks

So new beginnings rarely come all at once. Like April, they can be tentative and slow to emerge, as they gather energy and momentum, wash away the old and welcome the new.

When the Christian church first came to Britain, it had such a tentative beginning. As it began to weave itself into the spiritual life of the people, there was much mixing and merging of the old and the new. We are told that when Joseph of Arimathea came to Glastonbury, he rested on Wearyall hill and placed his staff there. During the night, it took root and became a blossoming hawthorn. Henceforth, it was known as the Glastonbury thorn, which ever after blossomed on Christmas day.

The Celtic Christian saints were wild men who lived alone in wild places. For them solitude was a sacrament, a path to wholeness. Yet we as a culture have abandoned this relationship with solitude, equating it only with loneliness and choosing instead to seek wholeness through relationship with another. When we rely upon another to meet all our needs we set the relationship up to fail. When we can meet our own needs, we enter relationship as whole individuals and can enjoy each other all the more for this. But meeting our own needs requires us to regularly spend time alone.

Loneliness hurts partly because of our tendency to polarize when in relationship. If I carry this and you carry that then when I am alone I will feel the hunger for what I no longer have. I will have to sit with my needs and I will long for you to come and meet them again. Being alone can be an uncomfortable place, it can compel in us all sorts of distracting and addictive behaviours. If we resist them, feelings emerge. Feelings perhaps of abandonment, shame and deep insecurity. Knowing this, even at an unconscious level, will make us fear solitude. The only way to overcome this fear is to face it.

There is an old story about a ship that arrived at an island in need of replenishment. On the island sat alone a huge giant and the sailors, despite their hunger and thirst, were too scared to go ashore. Only the cabin boy seemed unafraid so they sent him on ahead to negotiate with the giant. The closer he got, the smaller the giant became until at last they met and the giant was just a child. "Please don't hurt me" said the child. The cabin boy reassured him and then returned to the ship to tell the sailors that it was safe to land. They asked him the name of the giant and he told them that it was Fear.

So it is that the more we practice solitude, the more we learn about its twists and turns, its dark avenues and silent squares, and the less fearful it becomes to us. No longer a terrible giant. Just a small and frightened child on their own.

Once we overcome our fears of being alone we can find that with time it can become the least lonely place of all. Without distraction, without the pressing needs of others, we can enter into a deep and fulfilling relationship with ourselves, with Nature and with the Divine. The old saints applied meditation, prayer, simple sacred tasks and ritual as their practice. In meditation, in the still and silent contemplation of the breath, we can rediscover and revisit the great lake of peace that lies forever as a water table beneath all our fears and stresses. In prayers of asking we send deep affirmations to the higher self. In prayers of gratitude we give thanks for what we have at this moment, this breath, this morning, this family, this forest, these hands, this birdsong, and in doing so we undo the strands of negativity and fear that entangle our inner child and help them feel safe and bountiful once more. In simplicity we honour the sacred in all things; washing in the stream, shitting in the woods, picking blackberries, building a fire, drinking rainwater, laying ourselves down to sleep beneath the stars. In ritual we give voice and ground to all that emerges from our rested and contemplative hearts, and as we speak to Nature so she replies to us. As our senses learn the tone of her voice we find that solitude, like the heart, is not a still place, but an ever unfolding vision quest into the unknown. Into the landscape of the Soul.

But often the self alone does not yet have all the resources it needs to find fulfillment. The story of Olwen, she of the white track, tells us much about this. Olwen as a goddess is a personification of the divine feminine. She is our joy, our spring of wellbeing, our muse. She is our creative potential. To marry her we must be set by the parent the impossible tasks. This is an illusion. They only seem impossible because of the parent that sets them. They are the unspoken blocks to our wellbeing that have been conditioned into us by unconscious parenting. So we dare not allow intimacy, we dare not let ourselves shine in the presence of others, we dare not let our hair down and have fun, we dare not go wild, we dare not show anyone our art. The tasks therefore are to dare, and in the face of our conditioning they seem impossible. In the story Culhwych recognized his limitations and turned to the Knights of the Round Table for help. So we too must look for our knights.

Friendship is no accident. We are drawn to one another because we each have a little of what the other needs. We are seeking exchange and we can make this a conscious agreement. From whom can I learn to meditate? Who will help me to sing? Who will hold me when I cry? With whom can I go dancing? Who will listen to my poems without judgement? Who will run through the woods with me shouting? And the equally important question, what can I give in return? What do you need from me?

Perhaps it is partly for this reason that we have our stag and hen nights before the wedding, to rally and honour the knights that support us in our quest for the other. It is our relationship both with ourselves, found in solitude, and with others, found in friendship, that helps us complete the impossible tasks and prepares us for the wedding to come.

The hawthorn is a tree of the heart, love and fertility. In Celtic tradition marriages could only take place in the light part of the year and so they began at Beltane. The hawthorn was always used as garlands, especially for the bride and groom. By the end of April, it is a mass of creamy white blossom with a rich and sensual aroma.

The Celtic sun god Lugh created a partner for himself out of spring flowers. Her name was Bloduewedd and it is she that the May queen represents when she is dressed in blossoms for Mayday. The May king, also known as the Green man, wears hawthorn too.

This is a wedding of the sun and the earth and it heralds the fullness of spring, lush and fecund. But it is also an inner wedding, a marriage of the masculine and the feminine within so that we can begin truly to act according to our heart.

In silencing and unseating the bad advisor, the fearful self-obsessed, chattering mind that keeps us from our dreams, we open the door to a new masculine, soft and strong, protective and powerful. This is the inner groom, potent and earthy; he sings, dances, wrestles and roars. Unlike the chattering mind, he is deeply rooted in his sexuality and rides his power bareback through the woods. He is full of laughter and love. He climbs trees and jumps into streams. He is strong and sensual and he will fight for his beloved.

But there is also a parenting quality in hawthorn, cherishing the young, cleansing, guiding, nourishing and preparing the bride for the wedding to come. Because hawthorn opens the heart it replaces the stern, reproachful, neglecting parent with one who welcomes the passion and sensuality of spring. The culture that honoured hawthorn encouraged its young to make love in the woods as part of the Mayday festivities. This was a permissive and playful time, a time of rejoicing, a time of love. Many children were made on Mayday. It is this quality that walks beside us now and, under the spreading branches of the Oak tree, gives us away.

Here at the end of April as we prepare to break out of the egg and ascend to a new cycle of growth it is the love of self that we need. It is the time of the wedding between 'he who does' within us, to 'she who feels' within us. It is the time to look upon our selves, our soft and needy hearts, with the same gentleness, compassion and devotion that we feel for those that we love. It is the time to make vows of unconditional love and loyalty to ourselves. It is the time to ritually wash away the neglectful and abusive inner parents that have held our dreams in check for so long and replace them with our own inner bride and groom, beautiful, empowered and unashamedly in love.

Chapter 7   May

The Wedding

All around us now a great passion stirs in the land. The sun and the earth wrap themselves around each other like lovers. The days lengthen and grow rich and sensual, the sap is rising and the beast seeks his mate. The spirit of the Green man runs, released and aroused, through the woods and everything he touches rears up in wild abundance. The great ferns uncoil and stretch, like serpents in the sun. The wildflowers adorn the land like a scattering of jewels. The trees begin to drop their soft silks, their gentle rainbow blossoms, and enrobe themselves in rich and luxuriant greens. There are so many layers to this ocean of green, incandescent limes that blaze in the sunshine, deep velvet shadows full of turquoise, greens that shine and shimmer like glass, greens that sparkle like emeralds. The dam is breached and life floods out, unrestrained and joyful, surging like a great green wave from soil and bark, just as foliage tumbles from the mouths of the Green men that adorn our ancient churches. The fullness of spring is unleashed. Beltane is here.

Working in a small group together beneath the oak tree we weave crowns for ourselves out of blossoming hawthorn. Then we write our vows to ourselves, vows of commitment, love and loyalty. We make little gifts for each other out of the treasures that grow so abundantly around us now, gifts that honour the other, their strength and their softness. A bouquet of pheasant feathers bound to a stone. A daisy chain necklace with an oak leaf pendant. A little figure of clay and bone, wrapped like a papoose in dock leaf and cleavers. Then one by one we take turns to be wed to ourselves.

Each of us stands beneath the great oak and placing the crown upon our own heads, we read aloud our vows. Then the others step forward and present their gifts, explaining what they symbolize as each is given. Together we declare each one of us "married to yourself" and throw handfuls of confetti, spring blossom gathered from the hawthorn, the cherry and the apple. Then is the time for celebration, the lighting of the Beltane fire, the singing, the dancing and the feasting.

The Beltane fire is the Need fire and when we jump it together we state and honour our heart's needs. Once at a Mayday celebration for a little school we crowned a young king with oak leaves and gave him a drum. Then we crowned a young queen with hawthorn blossom and gave her a bell. Together they walked around the circle playing their music. The voice of the king, the drum, was strong and loud. The voice of the queen, the bell, was soft and gentle. So it is with the head and the heart. As we learn to hear and honour them both together the king and queen of the May lead us through a doorway of oak, under showers of petals and into the light half of the year.

Traditionally all weddings would take place beneath the oak tree. The oak flowers at this time, like soft green lace clustering among its leaves, and as the days go by it begins to fall upon us like confetti.

Coming home

With the arrival of Beltane comes the great surge of spring. The forests and hillsides are decked in fresh and sunlit colours and the song of birds and the buzz of insects is everywhere. The whole world feels new and freshly painted. It is as if we have stepped through the doorway and found our home renewed.

This doorway leads us into the light half of the Celtic year, so we bring with us much that was unconscious and in the dark into consciousness and into the light. As we do so we ascend with the vegetation to a new level of growth.

To the Celts this doorway was the oak tree. Its Celtic name Duir is the root of our word door and means solidity and protection. Castle doors were made of oak. They kept the enemy out and welcomed the beloved home. As we step through this door, there are lessons to be learnt about home, its boundaries and its openings, as well as the skeletons we keep in its dark and secret cupboards.

Home contains us. It is the outward manifestation of the feminine, an extension of the womb. It begins with our body and how we choose to dwell in it. Those emotional demons we choose not to face will find neglected chambers in our bodies from which to nag at us and make us attend to them. With the commitment of our masculine to honour, listen to and empower our feminine also comes a need to honour, listen to and empower our bodies. This can mean changes in diet and in lifestyle, as we endeavor to make our bodies into healthier homes for our souls to dwell in.

Beltane is a wedding and after this the groom, the inner masculine, must bring the bride, the inner feminine, home. This crossing of the threshold is deeply symbolic and we can honour these thresholds and doorways in our practice, marking or finding them in wild places. What do we have to lay down in order to carry ourselves over this threshold? What do we have to grieve in order to be free? It is here that we leave the parental home, with its secrets and shadows and seek to make a home of our own. The oak, a home to so much life in the forest, is a tree that evokes the gathering of the power within us, the lighting of the fire in the hearth. But at the beginning of May, often as not, all we can feel is our powerlessness. For in stepping through this doorway, we begin afresh and are reconnected to the child within and their experience of home life.

If the child within still resides in a neglected place, a place of shame, remorse or rage, then all journeys in our life will bring us home to that place until we find the courage to face it. If the parental home contained violence, neglect, abuse or abandonment, then we have probably spent half our lives trying to run away from it. But we will always find ourselves back there, in one relationship after another, until we return to that hard home within ourselves and free the child that we left there. Then we can carry her to a new home, a home of our own making.

Working in Nature, we can always find the old home again. This ruined stone wall with its hearth still intact, that copse of trees full of shadow and thorn. This cave on the beach with its bleached driftwood skeletons, that bog in the woods, sucking, entrapping, devouring. This moorland slope, barren and exposed, that hollow blasted oak, strong as a tower, dark as a tomb. Returning to the old home conjures up the spirits that dwelt there. Sitting with my back to you, I can become father, silent and aloof, and you can speak your home truths to him at last. Whispering words of judgment and condemnation from the trees, my voice can becomes mother's and you can find your voice there too, strong, enraged and claiming the last word as your own. Sometimes we need to make our parents and summoning our power, cut them down. Sometimes we must make the child that we were and stepping into a parental role ourselves defend that child from those that would harm it. Sometimes it is our siblings we must face, reclaiming aspects of ourselves that were given to them in the unconscious sharing out of childhood feelings, expectations and roles. Grandparents, friends and relatives, invaders and abusers, whoever met and hurt us in this place, they wait for us still. To be met again, and this time, overcome.

The oak tree stands at the centre of the year. It is a symbol of strength, resilience and the gathering of power. Known as the king of the forest, this most masculine of trees is a totem of both manhood and royalty. Yet it is the soft and aching heart of the oak that we feel here, as we leave the gentleness of hawthorn and step out into the open, revealed and vulnerable. The gathering of the power within occurs in reaction to this, a building of safe boundaries, a strengthening of spirit, a relighting of the fire in our heart. A good king needs a strong castle from which to rule, unbreachable from the outside but soft and welcoming within. Here at the beginning of May, we begin to build it.

Building castles

What child has not made one? Castles in the sand with seawater moats. Flood walls hastily raised to keep back the encroaching tide. Driftwood drawbridges, seashell windows, gull feather flags. Or find them on the sandless beaches, little prehistoric monuments made from flat stones like the burial chambers of ancient kings. Take your inner child by the hand now and lead them back to this old and familiar craft. Building castles in the wood, in the rotting stumps of old trees, castles of bark, moss and flint standing proud on stones in the river, castles among the branches of trees with bridges and walkways fit for fairies, castles of mud and straw clambering like an African village through the ferns, their turrets topped with shamanic ornaments, a bird's skull, an antler, a pennant of snakeskin writhing in the breeze. Castles teach us about boundaries, about what we keep safe and what we keep out.

Children build castles because children build boundaries, and what we build or have demolished as children remains our foundation for life, like the raised earth mounds of Iron Age forts. If we were bullied at home, by the oppressive needs of a parent's inner child, by the abusive anger of an unconscious elder, by the neglectful stance of an adult who cannot find it in their heart to treasure us, then by the time we go to school we will be rich pickings for those other bullied children who seek to claim their power back by abusing those more vulnerable than themselves. If our boundaries have been breached or inadequately raised, others will know, as surely as a predator can smell the fear of its prey. Vulnerability flies like a flag of surrender from our highest turret. Unconsciously, we invite invasion. A pattern has been laid down and we will live by it until we consciously seek to change it.

Castles rarely have just one line of defence. They have moats, drawbridges, portcullises, towers, walls, keeps and doors. Some of us only need a sniff of the enemy's camp fire and we are off, charging to attack. Others wait until the walls are being breached. Others retreat behind strong oak doors and hide away in the hope that the enemy will lose interest, but pushed to the limit might yet flare up like a fire cracker. Some of us are still standing helpless and open mouthed when uninvited strangers are in the inner sanctum, pulling down the tapestries and pissing on the bed. Where do you lay the line?

The Celtic name Duir was also the source of the word druid. The druids honoured the oak because it summoned down the power of Esus, their sky god. The Druids were known as the wise men of the oaks but they were not the only people who worshipped these trees. The oak is sacred to many cultures. Because the thunder gods favoured it, the oak was seen as an oracle and a shrine. The sacred oak grove at Dodona was the oldest and most revered sanctuary in Greece. Abraham met his angels under an oak. St Briget created a retreat called the Cell of Oak in Ireland, where holy women burned acorns on fires that were always kept alight. Herne the hunter was an oak god, an antler horned spirit who led the wild hunt. The oak is closely associated with the sun and the solar cycle. It is ruled by fire, so the godhead of the oak was akin to the godhead of the sun.

As May grows lush upon the land and spring gallops into summer, it is this godhead, the fertile and all encompassing solar power that we feel all around and within us.

When the sun and the rain are in balance this power is free flowing, wild and natural. So it is in us when our sword is both forged in the fire of our anger and tempered in the water of our tears. But here in May as we learn about our relationship with power, we often find that this balance is missing. We find that our use, abuse or neglect of our power has been defined by the old kings that ruled before us, from whom we have learned, or against whom we have reacted. The power that was wielded against us as children, when the oak within us was just an acorn holding all its potential for magnificence and abundance may have left us stunted and lightning struck. Afraid of our own anger we cannot forge our sword. Unable to control it or so cut off from our heart that we cannot soften it with compassion, then our sword is not tempered and may become an instrument of abuse. So legacies of control and abuse, or impotence and powerlessness, get passed down generation after generation.

As we step through the doorway of oak these issues of power, its use and its abuse, are brought into the light. It is the facing of these demons within us that make us into conscious adults. The castle that we seek to build is both strong on the outside and soft and welcoming within. It rules over its kingdom with a gentle and compassionate hand but it repels invaders with an impenetrable force. Only by becoming conscious of old patterns of power and control can we choose to change them and so not inflict our wounds upon others weaker than ourselves. Neither will we fail to defend ourselves nor fail to speak our truth when we need to.

Oak invites us to witness and honour the godhead within ourselves. Oak invites us to observe how power moves through us, and how we use it against others. It also shows us how the old kings have shaped us and how the little acorn within still holds potential for magnificence and abundance. For the inner child is not just a memory of the past, it is a totem for the future. It is an archetype of creativity, growth and wholeness that we can still tap into and draw from, transforming old patterns into new opportunities and opening the door to true and compassionate power.

Once we took photos of ourselves with an instamatic camera and then made shrines among the trees to the gods and goddesses in the photos. In each shrine we placed totems of their power, its use and its abuse. We celebrated their gifts and treasures but we honoured their shadows too.

Guarding the sanctuary

Every god and goddess needs a sanctuary, a holy place that cannot be desecrated under any circumstances. The oak is a home to all. Badgers, foxes and rabbits tunnel beneath its roots. Grubs, beetles, spiders and woodlice live beneath its skin. Owls and squirrels nest in its wounds. Birds live in its branches. Despite being considered a sacred tree, one could argue that nothing is sacred. Even the very heart of the oak can be ripped open by the lightning strike and occupied.

Our lives can seem like this, especially as we grow into adulthood and begin to take on responsibilities for others. When we open our heart to another we open the doors to the sanctuary within ourselves and invite them in. When we have children we do so again and before we know it our inner sanctum has become a family room. Sometimes that is lovely, sometimes not. When we need peace it can be crowded and noisy, when we need clarity it can be full of everyone else's junk. Sometimes we desperately need our own space, our own time, our own privacy, our own dreams, our own projects and there is nowhere at home or within ourselves to find them. Everybody else's needs are too pressing and our own too far down the list of priorities to warrant any serious attention. We wait for someone else to notice that we are struggling, but if we cannot prioritize our own needs, why should anyone else?

Often it is the many and pressing needs of the children that force our own off the list. As parents we must attend to these needs but if we sacrifice our own in the process we do the children a great disservice. Firstly we will not be well in ourselves. If our own needs are not met we will be stressed, irritable, depressed, and likely to snap at the smallest things. This will diminish the quality of our parenting and make their lives more miserable than need be. Secondly we will teach the children that the role of the parent is one of self sacrifice and when they become parents themselves they will have a tremendous struggle not to repeat this, as we all instinctively walk in the footsteps of our role models unless we consciously watch every step. So the legacy continues, generation after generation, and as grandparents we may see our grandchildren carrying a burden that we ourselves could have spared them.

It is the child, the acorn, which holds the answer. The oak is home to everyone but the acorn is home only to itself. Within the acorn is the seed of everything that is to come and the oak holds always the memory of the acorn within every part of itself. We too must reclaim this memory. In this holy place, this sanctuary, I am no one's partner, no one's parent, no one's anything. Here I am just me. Here there are only my needs to be met.

As we begin to seek this space within our lives we are inevitably accused of selfishness by those who have an investment in our old way. Selfish just means attending to self; it is our culture that has loaded the word with negativity and blame.

The sanctuary is the part of ourselves that we keep to ourselves. We may invite others to glimpse it or even step inside for a little while, but only those we trust in moments of love, and we always claim it back afterwards. Entry is by invitation only and any invasion is furiously repelled.

Even if we have a history of letting others trash our sanctuary we can start to guard it now. Even if the sense of it is unclear within us we will know when someone crosses the line. When we interact with another and leave feeling uncomfortable, disempowered or misused in some way then our boundaries have been ignored, probably because we were not asserting them adequately. If someone cannot see a boundary they will cross it. If we cannot be bothered to defend it then they will not be bothered to respect it. Sometimes we are so conditioned not to react that even when our discomfort tells us that someone is taking a liberty with us, we still cannot muster our fire. We leave feeling bullied and ashamed that we let ourselves down.

It is never too late to assert a boundary. If we come away feeling disempowered we will carry that feeling until we say something. Sometimes the anger comes later. Use it then. Speak to the other and tell them you are angry. In doing so you lay down a clearer boundary in retrospect and they will be more cautious next time. If this is not possible then learn from the experience and be more guarded in the future. Learn who the likely intruders will be. Practice raising your fire. Be ready. With time we can learn to speak our truth the moment we feel uncomfortable, the moment someone steps over our line. Then our sanctuary is safe.

When I was a child I was taught that I had to share everything with my younger siblings. So I made my private spaces in the garden, where I could lose myself in fantasy. I grew up believing that I had no right at home to any space or time of my own. Later when I began to seek retreat I would always find it away from home, in wild and natural places. But home remained a place of self sacrifice and consequently, paradoxically, I felt much less at home there than I did on retreat. Home, as they say, is where the heart is.

Then one day my wife and I were talking about this and she offered me our studio as a space of my own. To my surprise I found myself weeping, the child in me was so moved. Even then it took me many months to claim the space. When I did, I cleaned it out, repainted it and lit a fire at its door. Then I sat by that fire all night, keeping it alive until the dawn came. In time, when my son had grown up and left home, I took over his room in the house and the studio became a shared space again.

When we learn to keep a fire at the door of our inner sanctuary, no one will enter without invitation. When we learn to do this within ourselves spaces of our own begin to manifest outwardly in the world around us. All of us need a space of our own, a castle over which we can rule without interference from others. A room, a studio, a cabin, a tree house, a caravan, a hidey hole, a den. A place of our own to come home to.

The lightning strike

As the days grow longer and warmer and the countryside greener, we feel the power growing around and within us. By mid May the oak tree's foliage is lush and full and its shadowy realms buzz and rustle with life. These mighty trees, so aged and strong, have long been a symbol of power. But this power is tested. Of all the trees, none draw the lightning like the oak. When the bolt strikes, the sap heats up in a second to a thousand degrees, bursting the tree apart. Yet so many survive, great ruptured giants upon the land, doorways through which we can pass in ritual, symbols of resilience, endurance and strength. Throughout our lives we too draw the test to ourselves. When the lightening strikes, everything is in that instant illuminated. Our strength, our weakness, our courage, our vulnerability, all becomes visible. We learn our limits, the sweep of our power and that which we can endure.

Lightning strikes come in many guises. Illness, accidents, unemployment, separation, financial difficulties, bereavement, bullying, they inevitably test us in the arena in which we feel most vulnerable. We each have our own lessons to learn and we will be tested again and again until we learn them.

Often at this time we seek objects in the woods that symbolize the lightning strikes both past and present that have tested us and continue to do so. These we mark with a flame to show the burn. We share our stories of strikes past, how they hurt us and how they made us grow. Together we learn about the gifts that the lightning brings. This helps us sit now with the strikes present, with the tests that we now face and seek to endure. We combat fear with trust, self doubt with expectation. Then we make a fire out of all we have gathered. Standing together around the hearth we take turns to suggest ways of raising the fire within ourselves. We leap, we roar, we chant, we dance. We stamp our way around the circle shouting "Yes! Yes! Yes!" We stand in silence holding hands, drawing the heat into our bodies. Then we are ready. Ready to face our tests.

Because of its relationship with lightening, the oak has long been associated with the thunder gods, such as Thor, Zeus and Jehovah. These gods were intensely patriarchal, warmongering, vengeful and all powerful. They represent the masculine in its pure form, unsoftened by the heart. They connect us to our own fathers, to the father within us and to issues of power, anger and courage. They are heroic gods and they evoke and empower the hero within.

The Germanic hero Siegfried was the child of Siegmund, who left his son a great and beautiful sword. The sword was broken, but if mended it could never be defeated. When his parents died, Siegfried was raised by a dwarf. The dwarf had no love for the child, but intended to send him against the dragon Fafnir, in order to recapture the great hoard of gold which had long before been stolen from the dwarves and now lay beneath the serpent's coils. Then he planned to kill Siegfried and keep the treasure for himself. Siegfried was warned of the dwarf's treachery, so he reforged his father's sword and slew him. Then the young hero sought out the cave of Fafnir the dragon and overcame the beast. But from the treasure, he took only a helmet of invisibility and a magical ring, forged by the dwarves in ancient times and holding the power to enslave and create.

J.R.R. Tolkien borrowed much from this story when he wrote "The Lord of the Rings". The sword that is mended and the ring of power are both archetypal totems of the hero's quest. In our own fathering there may be elements of the cold or stunted father like the dwarf in this tale. The power that is our birthright is the sword that is passed down from the warrior that was slain, the father we might have had or perhaps glimpsed occasionally. We must overcome the stunted father in order to reclaim the warrior within and re-forge the sword that was broken. This is a symbol of the healthy masculine.

The ring is a container. It encircles the softness of the flesh just as the rings of the tree encircle the sapling within. It is from this centre, the heart of the oak, where dwells the archetypal child with all its potential and creativity, that power comes. It flows through the ring, and out through the hand that wears it. This is a symbol of the healthy feminine.

The ring is a doorway and it mirrors that through which we step now, from the unconscious struggle with our wounds to the conscious manifestation of all that we dream of. All around us now new life bursts out of darkness, as effortlessly as water pours from a cup. We too manifest our own lives as effortlessly but the reality we draw to ourselves can be shaped by the feelings that enslave us, the unconscious negative beliefs that we hold about ourselves and the self demeaning language that they inspire. So we may complain about uncaring partners and that is exactly what we get. We may obsess about debt and manifest more and more. We may bemoan the state of the world and the world that we experience becomes worse and worse. But these beliefs all have feeling at the heart of them and it is this we must find and release.

Our hero's quest is to name these spells and overcome them. The sword, our masculine, is the means by which we cut through the thorns that overwhelm us. But the ring, our feminine, has a power greater still. For by letting go of the feelings that bind us we can begin to manifest our dreams. Like the ring of power, it is feeling that enslaves and it is feeling that creates.

The cup that best defines the feminine is the Holy Grail. The wine, the blood of Christ, flows through its lips in exactly the same way as power passes through the ring. But until we have been tested we will not even recognise this grail, let alone be able to drink from it.

The knight Parsifal was so tested. As a young man, he found the Grail Castle where the Fisher king lay ailing and the land about lay in waste. Had only Parsifal the wisdom and compassion to ask the right questions, all would have been healed. But the foolish and proud youth said nothing and the castle vanished. For years Parsifal wandered and lost all remembrance of God. He took to violent deeds until at last he met a hermit who shamed him to tears. The hermit granted him absolution from his sins and Parsifal set out to seek the castle once more. Under an oak tree, Parsifal met a young girl and because he was kind to her, she gave him a magic ring. The ring led him eventually to the castle and there at last he found the Fisher king again. Now, older and wiser, Parsifal felt the king's pain as his own and asked the questions 'Lord, what ails thee?' and 'Lord, whom does the Grail serve?'. In the asking, the king and the land were healed.

The first question addresses the masculine. The grail castle is the place of safety, the therapeutic space, and when we find it we are invited to answer this question as truthfully as we can. What ails my masculine, my active self? Why can I not keep a job, stay in a relationship, make a living doing something I enjoy, stand up for myself, speak my truth, honour and meet my own needs? The second question addresses the feminine, of which the Holy Grail is the symbol. Who does my feminine, my feeling self serve? For whom do I carry these feelings? Whom do I seek to protect or shelter? What fears or loyalties keep me from my own needs? In whose service am I unconsciously bound?

These two questions form the foundation of the therapeutic process, for if the grail does not serve the self then we may become ill or dysfunctional in some way and remain so until we question it. But the seeking of the grail castle and the asking of the questions requires two things. The first is courage. To embark upon this journey of self discovery, to go willingly into the place of greatest resistance, to enter therapy or seek an encounter with one's wounds, is a hero's quest, regardless of gender. It is a sacred rite of passage and the means by which we attain conscious adulthood and come into our power. The second is wisdom. Parsifal failed the first time because he was too young. He needed the rough hands of life to push him around for a while and make a wise and tested warrior out of him. So do we.

Although we must re-forge our sword on the fires of the masculine, it is in the tempering of the blade in the waters of life, that we find real power. So we will be tested again and again until our metal is strong enough to overcome. This is our lightning strike, our illumination and our empowerment. It is our own hero's quest, as surely as were those sung by the storytellers of old.

Telling tales

Find three places in Nature, one for your experience of weakness and vulnerability, one for your experience of the lightning strike, and one for your experience of power. Now sit in each one and gather words, phrases and sentences onto paper that describe the things you can sense there, the sights, the sounds, the smells, the tastes, the textures and the things you feel inside. Then weave these lines together into something that flows, a poem for each of the three places inspired by the experience and all that shares the space with you. Then, in a group, read these three poems together, one after another. This is your hero's song.

But does life make heroes and heroines out of us just so we can look after ourselves? A castle is not there just to protect the king and queen. Once our sanctuary is sound and sure we have a sword to wield for the sake of all. In these times it is not just feelings about our own immediate lives that may need acknowledging. There may be causes that inspire us or raise the fire within us. We may be aware of injustice, cruelty or neglect in the lives of others and feel compelled to act on their behalf. Also, many of us grew up in a softer, greener world. Now that so many of the wild places that we loved have gone it may seem to us that our children have been robbed and deprived. What grief have we inside for the loss of the forests and beasts that inhabited our world and enriched our imagination when we were young? Stranger still, why is it often the case that we know it to be there but can not feel it?

When grief is so vast that the psyche cannot comprehend or process it the result is denial. How then can we expect to feel the pain of ecocide, the relentless mass destruction of habitats all over the world?

But if we do not feel it we cannot use our sword against it. Just as we must honour our own wounded feminine in order to find the power to change our lives, so must we honour the dark mother that rages and weeps in the desolate and abused corners of the world for she holds in her heart the power that we need to turn things around.

Our bodies and our instincts have evolved to nurture and protect our young. A woman's body has evolved to mother, it is soft and nourishing. If she is more feminine than the man it is to make her sensitive and intuitive to the needs of her children. A man's body has evolved to protect. While the woman feeds the baby he stands guard at the entrance to the home. If he is more masculine than the woman it is to make him more aggressive in the face of a predator.

But today's predators are man made. How can we defend our young against climate change, the loss of our natural habitats, pollution and its attendant cancers?

When ships were made of wood whole forests of oak were cut down to make the fleets that defended the kingdom. Now it is this desolation of the natural world itself that is the enemy. Once in May we made an elaborate archway over a stream and made little boats, in which we placed the feelings that we wanted to bring now into the light. It was lovely to watch these beautiful little vessels sailing through the doorway into consciousness. What can we do now to bring our feelings about the condition of the world into the light, where they can inspire and empower us?

If the oak is the father of the forest then the beech is the mother. Beech woods become lush and beautiful cathedrals in May as the canopy of soft green leaves spreads between their smooth and towering pillars. Beech feeds the whole forest with her leaves and her beechnuts, all of which can be eaten. The Celts associated beech with ancient wisdom, with the old stories that are passed down from mouth to ear and with ancient writings. This is the wisdom of the feminine, the wisdom of the heart, the wisdom of love, childbirth, healing, of Nature's ways, of dying and grieving.

Because they use metaphor, stories hold feeling. Mythology is like a recipe book for the heart, transmitting this wisdom across millennia. Beech woods invite the storyteller in each of us to emerge again.

A simple and affective way to create and share inventive and extraordinary stories is to collect a number of things from the forest. Let each person choose one and decide what or who it can be. It can be anything apart from what it is. This feather may be a beautiful girl, an eagle or a sailing ship but it cannot be a feather. This egg shell may be a carriage, the moon, or the eye of God but it cannot be an egg shell. Now in groups make up and perform stories, using these characters and things. In a large workshop we then ask each group to choose a favorite character from their story and make it as a sculpture in the woods. Then everyone walks the sculpture trail together and as we do so we join the characters together in a single group myth.

The small group stories often reflect interpersonal issues pertinent to the group that made it. But time and time again the large group myths speak of global and environmental concerns. When large groups of people meet together and work creatively, weaving metaphors together like yarn, the fabric that emerges often displays the face of the dark mother, our fears, our sadness and our rage at what is happening to our world. Regardless of our gender, race, special skills or special needs it is our common ground. When large gatherings of people or even whole communities make art, tell stories and enact ritual together they begin to bypass denial, release feelings and empower themselves to reshape the future.

The heart of the oak

Abuse and neglect can come in many forms. The violent hand, the rape of innocence, the angry voice. Emotional manipulation, criticism or cold intellectual distance. The absence of love, of gentleness, of care, of being held. Fear, deprivation, poverty, ridicule. A demon with many faces.

If we encounter abuse or neglect as children, and most of us do in some form or other, then we tend to recoil from the pain of it and may take refuge in the masculine, in keeping busy, striving and achieving, distracting ourselves from ourselves. The more we run, the more we find hiding places in the dark masculine where there is no feeling, and there we stand a chance of becoming an abuser ourselves. Children especially invite our attention because we are drawn to reintegrate that part of our self which was lost, the innocent child. Not only does the child draw us in, but the child's pain also. If we are unable to face the child's wound within ourselves then we may be compelled to wound a child in the same fashion, in order to revisit this place but from the perspective of the one

112

who had the power. We may find ourselves treating our children just as our parents treated us even though we hate ourselves for doing it. Something suffering within us is being drawn back to the feeling, even if we still cannot feel it ourselves, so that the opportunity for change and healing can reemerge. We are being called home to ourselves and if we do not find the courage to look within and own our pain, then another innocent may suffer and the legacy continue.

The men and women who abuse the innocent, do they not carry this shadow for all of us? We call them monsters but are they not the outward manifestation of the demons that lurk within each of us, the jagged edge of a cultural wedge of which we are all a part? If we ignore the demons within ourselves surely someone, somewhere will succumb to possession on behalf of us all. I remember in penny arcades as a child dropping pennies into machines in an attempt to push other pennies off the edge. In a culture that does not honour the shadow and is constantly pushing against its edges in order to feel it, should we be surprised when a penny falls? As long as our culture celebrates the masculine and represses the feminine we will be driven to push constantly against our edges in order to feel anything. So the media becomes more violent and pornographic, pornography becomes more abusive and abuse becomes more commonplace. Only a return to the feminine, to the honouring and release of feeling, can stop or reverse this process.

It is the same when Nature is abused. When the forest that we loved is stripped, when our childhood meadows become housing estates or when motorways carve our landscapes into portions we may recoil from the wounding that has been inflicted upon us and close our hearts. Then it becomes so easy to consume and pollute and waste, because we feel so numb, or at best just a little guilty.

When we hurt or disempower our children we may feel guilty too. But even guilt is a distraction. Look underneath and find the anger at those who hurt or disempowered the child in you. Look deeper still and find the tears. Keep searching and at the heart of the matter is always love. Love is the raw meat of the wound, the love that was denied, misused or unreturned and the love of the child, the innocent self suffering at the hands of the ones who should protect and cherish. This is the heart of the oak, raw and hot and aching, still living despite the lightning strikes, buried deep beneath the hardwood of years.

When we find our way home to this heart we re-enter the garden of our youth at the moment of our wounding and we feel the wound again. At this moment we step through the doorway into consciousness and into the promise of freedom. Here we can choose to end the legacy and release our children. This time as we feel the wound we understand it, and understand too that the abuser was also the abused, and being unconscious, was continuing the cycle. With this understanding comes the possibility of forgiveness. Forgiveness cannot be forced, it comes like the morning when the long night is done, but this deep knowing brings the morning a little closer.

Likewise, is it not loving Nature in her absence that makes us close our hearts to her? How can we endure loving the song of birds or the laughter of water when all we can hear is the hum of traffic? How can we endure loving the solitude of the wilderness and the wide starry sky when we live in the clutter of the city under a cold yellow fog?

But if we let ourselves feel and endure our love in her absence, we open our heart to the power for change. For love is the real power in us all that cuts through all others. Love inspires us to become warriors for all that we cherish. To protect our children, to protect our world and theirs. Love turns conscious adults into forces to be reckoned with. Love sends us into battle.

Chapter 8   June

Fire

As the days continue to grow longer and warmer, the sunshine and rain work together to weave a rich and vibrant blanket of wildness across the land. If we are lucky, the innocent warmth of the spring is replaced by hot and balmy summer days, but June is often wet and cloudy too and the forests thrive on all this water. The meadows and hillsides become jungles in their own right, lush with flowers, insects and wildlife. The ponds and streams come alive with water beetles, frogs and dragonflies. The chorus of birds is swollen by the arrival of the summer visitors, like the cuckoo, the house martin and the wild goose. The power that has been growing within the land is suddenly evident all around. Summer has come.

The astrological terms for the different states of an element are cardinal, fixed and mutable. The fire of spring is cardinal, emerging and growing. The fire of autumn is mutable, diminishing and changing. But the fire of summer is fixed, constant and blazing. It is the gathering of this fire in May and the expression of it in June that makes this the most solar time of the year.

The tree that the Celts associated with June was the holly. This is surprising as now we tend to associate this tree with Christmas. Yet if we observe the therapeutic process through the cycle of the year we will see again and again how the building of the fire in May is followed by its release in June. A fiery tree belongs here, a tree that honours the warrior within. No tree is better suited for this than the holly. This, the most armoured of trees, was perceived as the warrior of the woods and was named 'best in the fight'. Its Celtic name Tinne is the source of the word tinder and means fire. Charcoal made from holly was used to forge swords and axe heads. Holly was used as incense in the ritual consecration of knives. So holly stands at the most fiery part of the year, over the solar festival of the Summer Solstice. We bring it back in for

Christmas when its berries are full and red, to summon back the masculine after the long night of midwinter.

The holly represents the outward manifestation of the power that has been gathered inwardly in oak. In this respect, these two masculine trees stand side by side in direct relationship with each other in this the most masculine time of the year.

Just as oak attracts the lightning, holly has been known to repel it. Once I visited a farm that was recovering from a terrible lightning strike. The bolt had hit a fencepost surrounded on one side by holly trees and had flared across the ground away from the holly and into the roots of a great sycamore some distance away. Ninety sheep had been sleeping there and all had died.

So having drawn the power in, now we begin to use it, directing it outwardly upon the world around us. Summer is a very outward time and we need our power if we wish to pursue our dreams and strengthen our relationships within it. As the wildness grows in us all, it can be a time of great passions. The Bach flower remedies use holly to treat hatred, aggression, jealousy, irritability and thoughts of revenge. The heat is on and we are all cooking together.

This can be a very lively time, with places to go and people to see. The fire of holly fuels our activity and inspires our creativity. Yet here at the beginning of June, we may still be struggling to muster a spark.

In workshop we often make volcanoes at this time. Gathering armfuls of flowers, leaves or cut grass we sit in groups with our backs to each other. Then shuffling outwards on our bottoms we lie down so that the tops of our heads are touching in the middle of the circle and we place all that we have gathered on our tummies. This is the fire in our belly, waiting to be stoked up. Then we think of something or someone that has made us angry. As the feeling grows we begin to rumble, stamping the ground with our feet and banging with our hands. As it builds we begin to roar, adding our voice to the tumult and gathering up handfuls of our fire, ready to erupt. Then as we countdown from ten to zero, the roar grows in power, wildness and intensity until on the count of zero we explode, violently hurling our magma into the air and screaming at the top of our voices.

The wild man

The archetypal spirit of the holly is the Holly king. Perceived as a wild and hairy giant, clad in vegetation with a crown of holly and a huge club, he personifies the power that we keep harnessed within us, as repressed and disallowed anger. He is the rutting stag, the charging boar, the bear protecting its cubs. It is to him that we must go when we need our fire, to our inherent wildness, to our teeth and our claws, our spitting and our roaring, to the intolerable friction in our hearts that arises when we meet injustice, abuse or an obstacle in the path of our dreams. Without this fire we are impotent in the time of power.

His face appears everywhere, in the erupting vegetation of the hedgerow, in the stalking of the predator in the woods, in unresolved conflicts that suddenly rear their heads within our families, in drunken brawls on street corners. The wildness is in us all and it seeks release.

There is great healing in wildness. Most of the problems that face us in contemporary society, both personal and cultural, come from our separation from our innate wildness. Somewhere in the evolution of human consciousness we have forgotten that we are mammals first and have distinctly mammalian needs. The need for intimacy, curling one around another, hot blood and fur, the scent of our bodies entwined. The need for community, the loyalty and kinship of the pack, the thrill of the herd running as one. The need for parenting, the suckling child gathered to the heart, the teeth and claws held ready in their defence. The need for anger, the clash of antlers, the bone crunching impact of bull against bull, defending our loved ones, our rights, our homes and our selves. The need for grief, the pining and howling of the bereaved. The need for our natural habitat, to run barefoot in long grass, to climb trees and tumble into rivers, to feel the cold crash of waves upon our skin or the fury of a storm all around and within us, to sleep beneath stars on a bed of moss. Wildness is not just the snarling beast, the un-mown grass is wild too, swaying in the summer breeze and alive with grasshoppers, butterflies and spiders. The laughing stream is wild; the long cold night is wild, the shuffling hedgehog, the grass snake in the heather, the great dark fish suspended in the lake. We are wild too and our body remembers this even if our mind does not. When we take off our shoes and socks and step lightly upon the earth our body remembers. When we clamber up into the branches of a tree our body remembers. When we stand with our arms outstretched on top of a mountain and feel the wind sweep the lines from our face our body remembers.

So we look for our wild face in the woods. Sometimes we find it peering back at us, sometimes we make it. Great fearful faces on steep muddy banks, with teeth of slate and hair of bracken. Wild and wanton women leering and laughing up at us from the nettle bed. Satyr like men, horned and horny, stamping their hooves and bellowing their lust. Mighty, thorny warriors wielding their clubs and striding into battle. Wild and playful nymphs, nursing their secrets within the hollow halls of old decaying trees. Dark shadowy spirits hanging like genies in the cave's unseen heart. A presence, a suggestion, a half forgotten dream. When we find them we ask them what they need. Then stepping into their bodies, allowing their spirits to inhabit our breath, our eyes, our voice, we answer.

Usually, what the wild spirit desires most of all is release. A time and a place to be wild in, and the right to inhabit it. But there is so much fear in the way of wildness, because by virtue of its very nature, wildness feels unsafe.

When we try to make wildness safe, by turning the forest into a nature park, caging the beast or repressing our truth, we diminish ourselves and rob the world of its soul. When we try to save wildness for its own sake, by protecting the wilderness and defending our right to our freedom of expression, our mad and passionate spirit, our grief, our fury and our love, we enrich ourselves and give the world back to itself.

So our fears present us with new opportunities for growth, insight and empowerment. If wild things frighten us, the long dark night alone in the woods, the scuttling spider or sliding snake, the cold black depths of the ocean, the crash and bluster of the thunderstorm, the unknown rustle in the shadows, the stinking carcass in the bog, it is because they reflect back to us our own wild souls locked away in dusty cupboards, disowned, unrecognized and dreaded. Our fears box us in. As we meet and reconcile these aspects within ourselves we find we can climb a little higher in the tree, swim a little further out into the lake, raise our voice a little louder in conflict, cry a little more often in front of friends. We meet our fears and begin to feel safe with them. The world becomes larger and richer as the walls of our cell dissolve.

So holly calls upon us to evoke and honour the spirit of the wild man. It calls upon us to find his face upon the land and recharge our hearts from his fiery countenance. Holly calls upon us to release the wild man from his earthly shackles and let him run through us again, storming through the woods, the spirit of freedom incarnate, our wild and wonderful power unleashed.

Challenging the all father

In the summer holly berries are new and green unlike the fiery red fruit that we bring into our homes at Christmas to welcome the return of the solstice sun. The harsh and thorny evergreen foliage is growing afresh as well and the new leaves are soft and vulnerable. So we find within the summer holly, a tree renowned for its vigorous defensiveness, a soft and childlike quality. But the new is protected by the old, as holly's extensive armoury clusters around the new growth.

This is the purpose of anger, to defend and protect our vulnerability. Whenever anger rears its head sadness always lies hidden beneath, a hurting, fearful place that if allowed our anger will guard as faithfully as a dog. It is worth remembering this when someone snaps at us, or when we snap at them.

In the Norse story of the great wolf Fenrir we meet this raw and passionate power restrained by intangible, unbreakable bonds. Kept in this state, anger is a corrosive force that will eat away at our health, our self esteem and our relationships. But released, allowed and exercised, it becomes a force for transformation.

If we do not allow our anger off the leash occasionally then it may escape by itself. Uncontrolled and unconscious, it may devour all in its path. At the great battle of Ragnarok Fenrir escapes and kills Odin the all father. Odin represents the all powerful inner parent, the absolute law within. This enmity between the wildness that would break free and the voice that says 'Thou shalt not' is particularly heated at this time of the year.

The all father must be challenged for it is he that decrees that the wolf be shackled. He is a construct of all the authoritative voices, internal and external, that have ever restrained our natural impulses. He is vital for without him our wildness would be uncontained and we could not exist in community. But when he becomes all powerful and the beast is bound, we lose our passion, our instincts and our power. We can no longer act on impulse or flare up in the face of adversity, without first checking in with him, by which time it is too late.

So standing on the empty beach we may feel the wild impulse to strip off all our clothes and charge, whooping, into the sea. The all father says, for heavens sake, someone might see you. Challenge him.

Or having tea with an elderly parent who skirts around their true feelings with chit chat, we may feel the wild impulse to say "enough!" The all father says, don't be childish, you'll upset them. Challenge him.

Or face to face with the one we have secretly desired for years we may feel the wild impulse to lean forward and kiss them. The all father says you'll make a fool of yourself. Challenge him.

The voice that challenges the all father gives us permission to live. Sometimes that permission is all that is needed. Often at this time of year we give each other such permission. Moving across the land we take turns to suggest ways of releasing our wildness as we go. Rolling down the hill, piggy backs across the stream, crawling through the long grass, wrestling in the meadow, jumping in the lake, dancing around the fire, singing to the stars. In the heart of our wildness we find again, like the soft new holly clustering among the old, the child.

The challenge of midsummer is to shake off the thorny overcoat of the old self and reveal the soft green leaves of the new. In these weeks leading up to the longest day it is the final death throws of the old self that we feel. Its struggle to live, our sadness at its passing and our anger at both. As the fire grows within and around us it is good to glimpse the shadow within the flames, the stirring of grief as it uncoils like a salamander among the embers. For when our fire is spent, it is this that we feel, the sadness that lay beneath.

So Holly calls us to seek among the flames for the old skin that we are shedding. It is not an easy transformation. The less conscious we are, the more resistance we will meet. But entered willingly, the mid-summer fire is a place of purification, rejuvenation and rebirth. It is a place where the enmity between our wildness and our self containment can be resolved at last, where these two aspects of the masculine, the wild wolf and the all father, can learn to live in peace. The fires of mid-summer can be the place of liberation.

Making mischief

Fenrir was the son of Loki, the trickster. Loki was a mischief maker. Mischief is an essential ingredient in any concoction, be that a personality, a relationship, a community or an entire civilization, because

120

mischief turns the familiar onto its head, makes us question that which is written in stone and opens new doorways where before there were only walls. Mischief pulls at the loose threads until something unravels. When a relationship becomes old and stale a little mischief goes a long way. This might be our relationship with ourselves, with another or with an outdated belief system. Old habitual patterns can become relentless and self destructive, but the investment in keeping them as they are can be overwhelming; just consider, for example, our relationship with fossil fuels. Sometimes only mischief can sneak through, like a jackal through a hole in the fence, to reveal the truth hidden behind the facade.

In environmental arts therapy mischief is a renewable commodity that can be made as and when we need it. Everybody's mischief is unique to them. Red hot embers sizzling in a clay cup. Parcels of dung wrapped in dock leaves. A dead wasp on a stick, its sting erect. Now you have it in your hands what are you going to do with it? What needs shaking up in your world? What mischief are you going to make today?

Children are very good at making mischief and one of the ways that they express this is by pulling faces. As we grow into adults and the all father takes hold of us we tend to censor these in ourselves in order not to offend so it can be extremely liberating to practice this old skill again. When as a child the Celtic hero Cuchulain was taunted by other children his battle fury came upon him for the first time. One eye shrank back into his head and the other stood out on a stalk. His mouth stretched into a snarl that split his face from ear to ear. Blood spurted from the crown of his head. The children fled in terror.

Together in the woods we too can cultivate our battle fury. Glaring, snarling and grimacing at each other like Maori warriors. Flailing our clubs, stamping like Sumo wrestlers, shouting our battle cries. Using natural pigments we paint each other's faces. In pairs with our hands on each other's shoulders, we try to push the other out of the clearing. Meeting your power, I meet my own. As the coming solstice turns up the pressure we may find ourselves having to face up to all sorts of conflict and powering up like this gets us ready for the battle.

Working with a fire can be a great tool for learning to meet another's anger with your own. Make a fire and imagine that this is the anger that you must face. Now make an image of a child, your own inner child, and place it in its relationship to the anger. Is it hiding in the bushes, as far away as possible? Is it on the edge of the hearth, just bearing the heat? Is it right in the flames, being consumed? Now take it to a safe place and gather up some stones. In order to protect the child you must extinguish the fire with your own. One by one hurl the stones into the fire, shouting your truths. As each stone hits there will be an incandescent eruption of sparks. Keep your own fire fixed and blazing, keep hurling truths until you have put the fire out. This is just as powerful for confronting the anger we met as children, even though the abuser may have died or been softened by time. At last we can find our words, meet fire with fire, and overcome the old king.

Often we fear raising our fury because of the damage it might do untempered. But we do not need to abandon our grace, our gentleness and our compassion in order to rage, we just need to tether them safely to one side out of harms way. Then when the battle is won we can release them again to hold ourselves and the other amidst the tears.

Nowhere is this process better illustrated in metaphor than in the tale of Cuchulain's first foray. The young warrior wanted to prove himself so he set out to make some mischief. Driving his chariot to the fortress of the sons of Nechtan, who had previously killed more of the men of Ulster than were still living on the earth, he beheld a great stone pillar which wore a collar of iron. Upon this, in Ogham, was written a challenge to any man of arms who should alight there. Cuchulain pulled the pillar out of the ground and threw it in the river.

"Surely" said his charioteer "thou art seeking for a violent death, and now thou wilt find it without delay"

But as each of the sons of Nechtan came out of the fortress to confront him, Cuchulain slew them and strung their heads on his chariot.

Then driving home, still in his battle fury, he brought down sixteen wild swans alive with his sling shot and tied them also to his chariot so that they flew above him. Then he chased a herd of deer on foot and caught two great stags which he also made fast to his chariot. This is how he approached the camp of his King, Conor of Ulster, his face deformed by rage, his grace and his gentleness tethered safely to one side. When the Ulstermen saw him they sent out their women naked to meet him. In the face of the feminine he lowered his eyes and his weapons and the men seized him and plunged him in to a barrel of water to cool him down. The water boiled and the barrel burst but they held him still and again and again they dowsed him until his fury left him. Then they dressed him in fresh clothes and took him to the king to honour his deeds.

Cuchulain's chariot tells us much about the nature of ambivalence. In our dealings with others, especially our loved ones, we may seek to be as
122

graceful as the swan and as gentle as the deer but if the battle fury is holding the reins we will not be able to find our heart. In trying not to be angry we are likely to present as cold, defended and aloof. Sometimes we need to rage in order to clear the path for love.

Old king, new king

Another fiery plant that usually puts in an appearance in people's work at this time is the stinging nettle. By midsummer the nettles are huge and malevolent and great armies of them fill every available clearing. They present us with an imposing counter force that can fight back. Beating a path through the nettles as they lash back at us we are likely to get stung enough to get really angry, and the angrier we get the less we feel the stings (until after, when we've cooled down).

With the arrival of the summer solstice, the longest day and shortest night, the land becomes a pressure cooker and something has to give. The weeks leading up to this can be a time of great conflict, both within oneself and in relationships with others. Only the release of anger can clear this, just as only the summer storms that erupt and crackle above and around us can clear the mid-summer air.

Tradition tells us that the oak king rules the waxing part of the year, up to mid-summer and the holly king rules the waning part, up to mid-winter. These kings meet and fight at both the solstices. At mid-summer, the oak king is slain and holly ascends the throne. Oak internalizes the power, holly expresses it, so with the crowning of holly we are called upon to release our anger and break the tension. This is the Summer Solstice battle, where we must slay our old king and raise our new.

The old king is the old self, aspects of which may manifest both inwardly and outwardly. Whatever is within us that keeps us from our power needs to be met and defeated. It might be our impotence, our fear of anger, our lack of voice, our avoidance, our weariness and collapse, our self-distraction. Whatever it is, it rules us for its own sake and needs knocking off the throne. The old king often emerges in behaviour that reminds us of a parent, usually father or whoever held his role. We may meet this behaviour in another but more often than not we meet it at this time in ourselves. We find ourselves sulking, flaring up or giving away our power just like our father may have done and we hate it in ourselves. This is just as well. Only when we hate it enough will we confront it and shake the old man off our back.

Relationships with others that oppress and disempower us are also aspects of the old king, left over remnants of old parental legacies that we could all do without. This can be just plain bullying in which case it needs addressing head on and to do so ritually at first with an effigy of the bully can empower us to face the perpetrator. But the old king can also be more insidious and subtle, in learned patterns of relationship with our loved ones where we are taken for granted, neglected, disempowered or treated like children in small ways, too small to get angry with at the time but cumulative in the power that they hold over us. The gift of the summer solstice is that by turning the pressure up it makes these things harder to bare and pushes us into conflict. Then the air is cleared and we can find our love again.

So often at this time we make effigies of the old king and find them a throne in the woods. Then we choose a club and try it against a tree to see if it is strong enough. We set ourselves tests to power up in the face of battle, like beating a pathway through a huge bed of nettles (all the more challenging if you take your shirt off first) or ripping the ivy off a tree (for which the tree will be truly grateful). Then we march upon the enemy. Shouting our words of power we knock the old king of his throne and demolish the effigy. Then we take his place.

Beneath the anger, there is usually sadness and the truly effective encounters with the old king are those that end in tears because this changes things. It is this grief that craves release, which brings us again and again back into old patterns in the hope that release can be found there. The grief of the child held still in the heart of the adult, carried forth into relationship after relationship; the grief of other less conscious and more painful relationships; the grief of lost hopes, forgotten dreams and broken promises; the grief of old love getting in the way of the new. When we cry, we release ourselves from this and when we cry together, we begin our relationships afresh.

This is the soft new growth of the holly that emerges now, lush and vibrant, from the old. It is the inner child's fear or experience of oppression that keeps us from our power and the old king's way was to collude with this for safety's sake. The new king is born in relationship with the child. Swift to the child's defence, the new king protects our right to be, to play, to thrive, to achieve our dreams, to find joy and peace in the world. Wielding his wild man's club, the new king cuts through the old king's armies of negativity, restriction and fear. The new king carves our path home to ourselves.

Lionheart

Just as it is vital to challenge the all father so that the wildness of the wolf can be unleashed when we need it, so it is equally essential that we do not silence him altogether and lose his restraining influence. Without our power we are impotent, without our restraint we are dangerous. If we exercise our power unrestrained within a family then it is the child that suffers, not only the children of the family but the child within our hearts and the hearts of those that we injure.

In his rise to fame and fortune the Greek hero Heracles became increasingly unrestrained. The city of Thebes had been defeated by the Minyan army under the command of Erginus and had agreed to pay an annual tribute of one hundred cattle for twenty years. Heracles met the Minyan heralds on their way to the city to collect the tribute and asked them their business. They told him that they planned once more to remind the Theban king of his good fortune in not having had the ears, noses and hands of every Theban man cut off. "Does Erginus indeed hanker for such tribute?" asked Heracles who then maimed the heralds in exactly this way and sent them back home with their ears, noses and hands strung around their necks. Heralds were considered sacrosanct by men and gods alike so to treat them so was a deliberate outrage. When the Minyans marched in revenge against Thebes, Heracles ambushed them and slew Erginus and his men. When Pyraechmus the king of the Euboeans and a staunch ally of the Minyans heard of this he too marched upon Thebes. But Heracles defeated his army also and then, disregarding all the rules of war, he ordered the Euboean king's body to be pulled apart by two horses and left scattered and unburied. Such an atrocity caused great terror throughout Greece.

The Goddess Hera was disturbed by Heracles excesses and so as punishment she drove him mad. Mistaking his children for enemies he shot them down and flung their bodies onto a fire. When he came to his senses he was overcome with grief and shut himself away. Then he went to Delphi to consult the oracle. The Pythoness told him that he must serve Eurystheus, a weak and cowardly king that he despised, for twelve years and perform whatever labours the king should ask of him. This he did and his reward was immortality.

Only the dark feminine, in this case a vengeful Hera, can stop an unrestrained masculine. Is this not what we meet now in the devastation caused by global climate change, in the floods, the storms, the extreme temperatures and chaotic seasons? Any culture that dedicates itself wholly to the unrestrained pursuit of the masculine, to material gain, to power, to exploitation and to progress at any cost will become dangerous to itself and will eventually drive itself mad. Once again it is the children that will suffer, for the world that we are leaving for them promises to be a much hotter, harsher place. Before we cast them onto this fire, we might choose to consider what our labours might be.

The way of the old king is to collude and allow things to worsen. The way of the new is to defend the feminine in all its manifestations. To the new king the feminine is the Holy Grail, it is sacred and to be protected at all costs. So feeling is sacred. All wild and natural places are sacred. Childhood is sacred. Elderhood is sacred. Biodiversity is sacred. Indigenous populations and traditions are sacred. The feminine, with all her many faces, is by her very nature extremely vulnerable and at risk from exploitation, neglect and abuse. The unrestrained masculine will always gather its power at her expense, be it the abusive adult in the family, the money hungry corporation or the war mongering government. What is more, the unrestrained masculine can always justify its actions because it is first and foremost a creature of reason. It will act in the name of progress, good business, the state, tradition, the good of all, even God. But it is its disconnection from the heart that makes it dangerous for in this way it can justify anything, from child brides to extermination camps, from the destruction of ancient forests to strategic nuclear war.

This presents us too with a new model for manhood. The traditional model was all masculine and no feminine. Then the new man surrendered his power to find his feelings but was left emasculated and impotent. The whole man has an equal balance of softness and strength. Heracles wore the skin of a lion but it is the lion in a man's heart that makes him whole. What use is a man's courage if he cannot muster it to face his own feelings, cry in front of other men, face the shadows within and release the grief of his childhood, share his softness and vulnerability with women, speak his heart's truth to his aging parents? The lionhearted man has the courage to honour and release his feelings however challenging they are, but does so in a way that does not abuse others. He can be soft and broken when he is held by those that love him, but when faced with the unrestrained masculine and its atrocities he roars and rages like the storm. He is the defender of the feminine, both within himself and in the world around him. He is a whole man, a lionheart.

126

Each of us can make this choice now, to collude and allow things to worsen or to take personal responsibility for our collective excesses and accept our labours. This will mean different things to each of us, but essentially change begins in the heart, moves out through the relationships within the family and close community and then sends its ripples out into the world. So when we commit to this hero's quest, confront our own wounds and seek an end to the legacies of old kings and queens, we begin a process that holds the potential to change the world. Never was the term "think globally, act locally" more personal. If we begin with the wounded self, with the immediate locality of our own heart, then we begin to turn things around from the inside out. We empower the feminine to manifest change. Then, as we become truer, stronger and clearer we can find our labours in the outside world. We can change the fuels that we use, the lifestyles that we live, the standards that we expect. Seemingly impossible problems find their own solutions. Heroic efforts are made on a day to day basis. Things change.

Shining

The midsummer solstice marks the longest day so it is a time to shine. Often in our celebrations, having cast totems of the old self into the fire, we seek to burn as brightly as we can ourselves, singing, dancing and making music together, improvising wild and free beneath the long evening sun. Releasing the archetypal child within ourselves, we can become incandescent.

To shine is our birthright and if a child is loved unconditionally they will do so freely and often. But conditional love or no love at all, will place shades around us and hide our light from the world and from ourselves. We will fear our own shining in case it should bring unwanted attention, judgement, condemnation or criticism. Or we may fear that we cannot shine or that if we should, our gifts would be squandered, wasted or go unacknowledged. The dream of our one great moment of incandescence becomes so precious to us that we dare not risk it for real, for whom would we be without the dream? So we never really try to write the book, paint the painting, build the house or travel the world. Instead we keep it on hold so that our potential at least is unbounded and can sustain us. But the price we pay for this is that we creep around in the shadows of ourselves and never really shine. In order to keep the dream of the butterfly alive, we stay caterpillars forever.

When the Celtic sun god Lugh first made himself known at the door of the royal palace of Tara, the doorkeeper told him that only those that excelled in a particular skill could enter there. Lugh said that he was a carpenter. "We have one of those" answered the doorkeeper. "Then I am a smith" said Lugh. "We have one of those too" replied the doorkeeper. "Then I am a warrior" said Lugh and again he was told that they had many of those. Lugh went on to name all his skills: a poet, a harper, a physician, a man of science and so on and each time another with that skill was already in the palace. "Then ask the king" said Lugh "if he has in his service any one man who is accomplished in every one of these arts and if he has I will stay here no longer" Upon this Lugh was admitted and the king was so impressed by him that he stood down in his favour and gave him the throne. Later, when Lugh appeared fully armed in front of the Danaan chiefs, they thought that they were beholding the rising sun.

Lugh is an archetype of accomplishment, success, abundance and well being that stands at the door for each of us, waiting to be let in. As the doorkeepers to our own hearts we can stand in his way forever, asking him again and again what right has he to enter. Or we can turn our energies against those parts of ourselves that seek to keep us small, quiet and safe and so clear the path for Lugh. As we embrace him we allow ourselves our excellence and he takes the throne. The shades fall from us and at last we truly shine.

Often, however, the spells that keep us from our shining selves are hidden, buried deep in the strata of our lives, dark reservoirs of shame, forgotten, neglected and untapped. If we wish to become all that we are then we must search for these lost veins of feeling to honour and release all that we find there. Once our midsummer battles have been fought we can sink back down into ourselves, back into the feminine and begin once again to intuit the deep undercurrents that stir in the heart of ourselves. As the storms pass the waters clear. Peering in, we begin to see.

The dark pool

Nothing contemplates stillness quite like a hot July day, when the summer settles down among the trees and meditates upon itself. The air is so full of sunshine it glows like amber and the tall grasses and flowers on the meadow stand motionless as if preserved within, while shoals of sparkling midges rehearse their mysterious dances overhead. Butterflies sail by like little kites unstrung and Bumble bees bumble in and out of the shadows. The birds can be strangely quiet as if they too rest in contemplation. Up above buzzards cruise the thermals, slowly and silently turning great spirals in the sky, watching with eyes as sharp as glass.

Lie in the long grass and the grasshoppers settle on your skin like tourists on the beach. Big shiny beetles amble by like armoured cars patrolling the undergrowth. Turn an old log and if you are lucky unveil a slowworm, a burnished copper bracelet that uncoils and slides away. Here and there strange chrysali hang beneath leaves like the sarcophagi of aliens, waiting. Within, shadows stir. Down in the pools, on the water's edge, the newts sunbathe just beneath the surface and the frogs try out their new legs. Dragonflies unzip themselves from their swim suits and linger in the sunshine, letting their wings unfold. Even when the days are overcast, wet or windy, there is a dreaminess to July, an expectation, a sense of something about to emerge.

After the fires of solstice have burned low, stillness descends upon the countryside, the peace after the storm, and we settle into the constancy of summer. Having fired up and fought our battles, we sink now back into the feminine, the dark pool of feeling that underlay our conflicts. As July begins, we start to sense these deep and hidden undercurrents and tentatively dip our toes in them.

The tree that the Celts often identified with this time was the Hazel. Known as the Celtic tree of knowledge, the Hazel was associated with wisdom, intuition and creativity. Hazel rods were used for divining water and minerals and so it helps attune us to the deep undercurrents within the earth and within ourselves. The metaphor associated with Hazel is the dark pool, the cauldron of the unconscious, the source of wisdom and inspiration.

Irish legend tells us of Connla's well, over which nine Hazel trees produced flowers and nuts simultaneously. These are, we are told, the hazels of wisdom, or of the science of poetry, and as the fruit and the blossom fall into the well together they raise upon the water a royal surge of purple. As the nuts sank into the water, the salmon that lived in the well ate them. Some say that this well is under the sea and that it called the father of all salmon to itself in order to give to him its gift of wisdom, and this began the annual migration of salmon to the sea and back. In the Irish story of Fionn, his druid master caught this magical salmon and intended to eat it in order to receive its wisdom. The boy was told to cook the fish but not to taste it. While doing so, Fionn burnt his thumb on the salmon's skin and automatically put his thumb in his mouth to soothe the pain. Instantly the wisdom of the salmon flooded through Fionn and he was conscious of everything that was happening in Ireland. The gift of far-sight was Fionn's and he became a great man.

We too must burn ourselves on the fires of the Solstice in order to receive the wisdom that lies beneath. This wisdom has always been there, it is the womb from which we are born and the grave into which we descend. We may spend our lives trying to swim away from it but it calls us back to itself, year after year, like Connla's well calling the salmon. Our wounds lead us down to it yet we fear such a painful descent, such a path of tears. But the still deep waters at the bottom are the waters of life, as boundless as the ocean and as infinite as death. When we bathe in these waters, we see at last the impermanence and interconnectedness of all things and find the great peace that lies beneath.

But why, when this wisdom is our birth right, do we allow our minds to fill with stress and clutter that keeps us up and out, in the bright illusion of our lives? The Tibetan Buddhists speak of four faults that keep us from this wisdom. They say that it is too close to be recognized; too profound to fathom; too easy to believe and too wonderful to accommodate. So we blinker ourselves like the plough horse and push on down the same old furrows oblivious to the wonder and spaciousness around. But all religions remember this place. The Celts called it

Gwynvyd meaning Godhead. This deep wisdom is a universal concept and an experience available to all.

It is our incessant activity that helps to keep us from this wisdom, the thrashing of the salmon that swims upstream against the current, fighting rapids and leaping up waterfalls in order to breed and make its mark in life. But once the battle is fought and the spawning done, then the salmon lets go. It allows the waters of life to carry it home, answering the call of Connla's well, back to the great abyss of the ocean.

So this is a good time to work on the water's edge. Sitting in silence we feel into the deep shadows within and sense the life there. Something moves, twitches, unfurls. In the blink of an eye a presence lets itself be felt. Using mud, gravel, sand, weed and shells we begin to make its image.

The people of poetry

The sun god Lugh was one of the Tuatha De Danaan, the people of Dana. This race of deities invaded and colonized Ireland but despite their mysterious and wonderful powers they were themselves ousted by the sons of Miled, a mortal race from across the sea. It has been argued that the reason for this is that the early Christian storytellers could not allow a pagan race, endowed with divine powers and characteristics, to be the progenitors of a Christian Ireland so they supplanted them with the Milesians, an equally mythical but wholly human invader, to which all of the dominant families of Ireland traced their descent. But at this point something interesting happens. Rather than be eradicated and forgotten, the Danaans cast over themselves a veil of invisibility and from henceforth there are two Irelands, the earthly and the spiritual. Where humans can see only green mounds and ruins now rise fairy palaces bathed in eternal sunshine wherein dwell the Danaan people in undying youth and beauty. So the ancient gods of Ireland become the people of the Sidhe (the fairy mounds), and although they have dwindled in power and status they remain a vital ingredient in the mythology of Ireland, living alongside the mortal world and stepping in and out of the business of men at their whim.

The name Tuatha De Danaan means the people of the god whose mother is Dana. This god has been named as Ecne, or poetry. So the Danaans were the people of poetry whose mother was the divine feminine. Suppressed by a patriarchal culture, they do not disappear, but rather slip into the background, where their influence upon human affairs becomes more subtle and mysterious. This myth tells us much about the secret world of the feminine. Less concrete and tangible than the masculine, it nevertheless underlies everything that we are, and its influences bubble up to guide, bewitch, entrap or empower us. It is everlasting, transcending the cycle of life and death. It is magical, obeying its own laws, not ours. It is a place of illusion and mystery, but deeper still it is the font of wisdom, inspiration and enlightenment.

The defeat of the Danaans does not mean the end of poetry. Indeed the Milesians themselves were led by a poet, Amergin, and it is he that first negotiates with the Danaans, for poetry is the language of the feminine. When Amergin first set foot upon the soil of Ireland he chanted this poem.

I am the wind that blows over the sea

I am the wave of the ocean

I am the murmur of the billows

I am the ox of the seven combats

I am the vulture upon the rock

I am a ray of the sun

I am the fairest of plants

I am a wild boar in valour

I am a salmon in the water

I am a lake in the plain

I am the craft of the artificer

I am a word of science

I am the spear point that gives battle

I am the god that creates in the heart of man the fire of thought

Who is it that enlightens the assembly upon the mountain, if not I?

Who telleth the ages of the moon, if not I?

Who showeth the place where the sun goes to rest, if not I?

Amergin's words come from the dark pool of the collective unconscious where ego is transcended and all things are one. Hazel was called the poet's tree, for poetry, the voice of the feminine, draws upon the deep reservoirs of the human heart as its source. When we go into Nature with a sense of the interconnectedness of all things the face of Nature herself becomes the shining surface of the dark pool, in which we will always see ourselves reflected. Poetry allows us, through the language of metaphor, to evoke and share this experience. Wherever we look, whatever we are drawn to, if we allow ourselves to open to the metaphor, then we will always meet an aspect of ourselves. As we have seen, just as stone is the foundation of the physical world, metaphor is the foundation of the metaphysical world, so metaphor is the philosopher's stone, a source of infinite wisdom and transformation. Not just because we can observe these aspects of ourselves reflected in nature, but also because we can interact with them. By externalizing the internal we can communicate with the gods that rule us. We can transform, understand, awaken and overthrow them. Poetry can lend great depth and insight to the voice that draws upon this power.

The hazel tree was sacred to the god Mercury or Hermes, and the atmosphere around a hazel is often described as mercurial. There is an old saying that silver snakes surround its roots. Mercury was the messenger of the gods. His is the dialogue that occurs now between our rational selves and the wise and knowing voices that whisper from the dark well of our unconscious. His staff was intertwined with snakes, the caduceus, the symbol of healing. So as the struggle of the Solstice recedes into the past, we can rest by the dark pool, lick our wounds and let them heal.

Poetry in itself can be intensely healing, because it can give us words for the unspeakable. When I first began going out into Nature to follow like a hunter the tracks of my feelings, it was poetry that so often allowed me to capture and hold the emotion, despite its intangible, fairie quality. Sitting alone by a stream I would let the words tumble like water onto the page. In the shadow of great trees I would feel them pushing up from the darkness beneath. On the cliff's edge they would swoop and dive, in the long grass they would creep and rustle, by the fireside they would crack and blaze. When the words felt right I would read them back to myself and the words read aloud would evoke the tears that I sought. The feeling would arise and overflow with them, sometimes like a great flood, as if the words had broken the spell that had sealed the door to my heart. Feeling, sometimes so old and hidden that I had no real idea of its existence and of its power over me until that moment, had at last found its voice and been released. No longer unconscious, it could no longer bind me.

Anima

The gift of poetry is its direct relationship with the feminine. As we begin to explore the hidden parts of ourselves its gives us the means to express and relate to them. However repressed and wounded they may be we can at last begin to define them:

Here I be

Anima

No daisy meadow virgin me

Old and buggered like a stunted oak I am

Burst and blackened by the thunder's tongue

Kept small, flat, nigh dead but never quite

My nose in the earth

I breathe her fluids like a fish

Whenever I am working with feeling, regardless of whether it is another's or my own, I always seek the words that hold that feeling, for our words carry our heart's pain out into the world. However stifled and silent they have been until now, we can at last give them a voice:

These

Are

My

Words

If I had a throat it would stretch like a pelican's

To relish their resonance

Roll them around like marbles in a jar

Spit them at the sun

And watch them dip and whirl like swifts upon the air

Beloved words

My poor and darling voice

Our voice should be beloved to us, but so often it is kept under lock and key. It is the freedom of form that poetry lends to us that loosens and frees the tongue. But in the unlocking, shadow can be evoked and awakened for one of the reasons that our voice is imprisoned is to keep it from giving substance to our horrors. So poetry can let us speak our darkest fears and face our bleakest nightmares:

When she opens her eyes ours fill with clouds and our skin bubbles black with the cancer of her gaze

When she opens her mouth there screams forth an ancient wind that rips open our cities like burst wounds

When she opens her womb the waters wash upon us and carry off our lives like driftwood on the flood

When she opens her heart the ice mountains melt and the deserts spread like burns upon the skin of the world

This is the way of Grandmother Bones

There is no mercy for matricidal man

This is our Halloween

Our long night begins

By expressing our sense of helplessness in the face of such horrors, poetry separates out the fear that can bind and paralyze us and places it upon the page where we can acknowledge and honour it, but no longer be at its mercy. Once we have stepped back from fear we can engage with any situation, however overwhelming, from a fresh perspective. Here the other voices, such as hope, trust, acceptance or valour, can begin to emerge. In this way poetry can even enable us to face up to our mortality:

So what's the point in hiding?

Every time I look in the mirror my face looks more like yours

You are the placenta that connects me to this dark and vibrant earth

My pale brother

I come to you now

Across the endless deserts of depression I come to you
From the dewy imprints of lovers in the meadow I come to you
Over mountains of fear and oceans of regret I come to you
From the splash of laughter in the glades of pleasure I come to you
Through forests of Rowan abundant with promise I come to you
Freely now among the dancing midges I come to you
I betrothe myself to you
Be my partner now in all things beginning

For death is ever present and growing older requires us to make our peace with it. My wife is a therapist who has specialized in working with elders who have Alzheimer's disease and related illnesses. Some of the most inspiring work that she has done with these groups has been with poetry. This has proven to be a powerful media for two reasons. Firstly because poetry read aloud lends eloquence and meaning to feelings that are evoked within the group process and then provides a vehicle for the whole group to share in that feeling experience. Secondly because poetry helps people who are endlessly seeking, striving, stuck and fixated to become present, reconnect to the bigger picture and find the voice of their inner elder once again. Individuals who are very distressed and isolated can find in a shared poem common ground with all the members of the group and move on beyond chaos to a place of deeper knowing, a place of grace and redemption, an awareness of the soul's higher purpose. From out of the mists of confusion, deeper, more enduring feelings are remembered and reclaimed, memories of joy, wildness and sorrow, freedom, courage and surrender, and most especially memories of love:

Only now can I fathom the impact of you
You who fell from the sky like a blessing
Unexpected, unaffirmed, mysterious
Yet perfect and inevitable
As only grace can be
136

Tumbling into my heart
You dipped your roots in the lake of my longing
And grew me a forest to walk in

But poetry also honours the love of self and the union of the opposites within us as we endeavor through our life's journey to find wholeness within our own hearts.

Still
Kay puts up her hair with ribbons now
And sleeps among the roses, smiling at the stars
And through a door she found unlocked
There is a hall with ribs of bone
So vast that eagles fly among its vaults
And there she dances, shouts and sings

One day he'll come
His cloak of wolf skin matted on his back
His shaven head, his dark and weathered face
His burden cast aside, he'll leap upon the wind
And scale the doorless wall
And down among the lions he will rage
And thunder 'till they curl up at his feet
And such a fire he will build
To melt that gate of iron

He'll lift her in his arms
And carry Kay into the world
And she will be the heart in all he does
And he will be the power in her love

From this union is born the archetypal child, our means of rebirth in the midst of all endings. Because poetry speaks the language of metaphor it brings us home time and time again to the secret and hidden world of the child within for metaphor is the very substance of play and transformation. By reconnecting us to this, poetry helps us to reconcile parts of ourselves lost since childhood:

In the soft crook of a tree
I found him again
My silent brother
Grown old from waiting
For me to come home

He looked with wonder at my grey beard
And I at his
And I tried to tell him of the years that have passed
But speech could not encompass them
So we sat in silence
And I wept for the child in the garden
And the parting of sweet ways

And when the work is done and the feminine released, poetry allows us to honour and celebrate her:

So here I be
Anima
The scent of woodland garlic on the breeze
The sunlit ember of a robin's breast
The wrenching of a pheasant from the grass
The stirring of a carp within the lake

The flowering of sorrow in a heart

The sound of children laughing in the woods

The nervous cunning in a fox's eye

The downy stillness in a lover's arms

The mother, daughter, bride of all

Resplendent in my summer robes

Afresh at last upon the wind

And free

The place of greatest resistance

By the end of July, summer is reaching its fullness and the air is alive with little angels and dragons, the butterflies having emerged from their chrysalis cauldrons and the dragonflies having risen like Lazarus from their dark pools. On the lakes and ponds the water lilies are in flower, exquisite symbols of transformation on the surface of the deep unconscious self. We too may be sensing this, feeling our new wings unfold. Transformation offers us freedom from old ways. It lifts the veil of illusion that restrains us and welcomes us into new possibilities. Those of our hopes that we have adhered to begin to manifest around us as if by magic.

In the Hans Christian Anderson fairytale Thumbelina, a little girl no bigger than a thumb is found in a flower and adopted by a woman who raises her as her own child. Thumbelina is stolen by an old mother toad who takes her to her pond, intending to marry her to her son. Although she escapes, she has to live underground with a mole in order to survive the winters, and the mole too wants her for his wife. Thumbelina finds an injured swallow in the mole's tunnel and she nurses it through the winter. The following year, the swallow returns and carries Thumbelina away to a land of perpetual summer where the little people live in the flowers all around. There she meets her true prince.

The toad is a denizen of the dark pool and speaks to us of all that we find base and shameful within ourselves. When we dip into these places we can find much feeling there, our child feminine secretly wed to unwelcome suitors, beset by toads or foraging blind with the moles. However much we struggle to manifest our dreams, we will always feel this weight bearing down upon us if we leave our feminine, even as much as a thumbs length, down in the swamp of our shame. But if we honour and release these feelings then we too are honoured and released. Then when we care for and nurture our dreams, like the swallow they return upon the wind to carry us away.

Shame can be the hardest part of ourselves to face and when we encounter it in Nature we usually find it repulsive. The stinking carcass of a dead sheep, a stagnant bog, a pile of decaying rubbish tipped in the woods, a derelict shack smelling of cider and piss, a rusty old tank full of black mosquito infested water. Rather than interact with it, all we want to do is run away. But it is exactly this compulsion that informs us of the importance of this find for this is the place of greatest resistance.

As a therapist I spend a lot of time leading people to this place and helping them to enter. No one wants to go there. Usually we arrive here together after a long therapeutic journey in which time, experience, empowerment and trust have combined to strengthen their resolve and their courage sufficiently enough to face it. There is always great feeling here, and at first it feels unbearable. This is the power of shame, it compels us to avoid it at any cost and so it can never be unveiled and seen for what it is. For shame is full of illusion. Once we make or face its image, speak its words and cry its tears then we begin to understand its true nature and it loses its power over us.

Shame can come from many sources but usually we can trace its passage back to childhood. If we were treated with disdain, contempt, coldness or aggression or if the love that should have been ours was directed somewhere else, or if blame was heaped upon us for someone else's unhappiness, then we probably still carry the shame for this. As we begin to sense its true nature and understand its origin we see that it was not us that behaved shamefully. Even if we were ridiculed for our looks, manner, family or social standing and consequently still feel sensitive about these things, we can now feel the anger at they that made us feel ashamed. The turning of shame into anger is extremely empowering. By giving back the shame we release and accept ourselves. We gather up the shamed child and take it from this terrible place.

Hazel speaks to us of self-forgiveness, of allowing the toads to be toads, of not avoiding the dark pool but allowing its lilies to flower instead. All that is beautiful, magical and wise comes from this cauldron. This well is deep. It takes us all the way down to our fear of death and to the grief of our own still to come. When we cry these fears, then we can truly begin to live.

Behold yourself

The gift of intuition, wisdom and insight can make us great mediators in times of struggle. As a source of creativity it can inspire both ourselves and those around us. Hazel can help us to become a catalyst, inspiring change in our own lives and in the world in general. As long as we remember to stop and be still and to listen to the quiet voices within. Finding times for stillness and reflection, especially in the middle of summer, can be hard. The creative urge drives us out into the world and this is often seen as a time for travel, holiday, festivals and parties. It feels good to fly like Mercury upon his winged sandals from one experience to the next, enjoying the sense of freedom, of being alive and inspired. But if this is all that we do then we can stop listening to our hearts and lose our connection to the very source that inspires us. Only in stillness and silence, in the act of being, feeling and receiving, can we access this source. So the task is to strike a balance, to find time to be both inward and outward. Otherwise we drain ourselves dry. In the twelfth century, the Christian mystic Bernard of Clairvaux wrote

If you are wise, you will show yourself as a reservoir rather than as a canal, for a canal spreads abroad water as it receives it. But a reservoir waits until it is full before overflowing and so gives, without loss to itself, its super abundant water.

In being, feeling and receiving we allow our reservoir to fill.

Nature has many ways of refilling us. When we awake to the glory of a beautiful sunrise she fills us with hope. When we play like children in the waterfall she fills us with joy. When we answer her thunder with our own she fills us with power. When we kneel by the river and surrender an image of our lost one to its currents, she fills us with grief. When we sit with the wisdom that comes from seeing and understanding our journey, watching swans gliding in silence on the dark lake, she fills us with reverence. And when the work is done and we stand alone on the hillside beneath the stars she fills us with grace.

Nature refills us with herself because Nature is the outward manifestation of our own feminine. Anywhere we go, anything we meet, it is ourselves that we encounter. A lovely exercise to honour this involves leading another around with their eyes closed. When we find something of interest, a cluster of lichen on a branch, a decaying log covered with fungus, a beautiful view across the valley, the sunshine sparkling in the leaves above, we turn their face towards it and say "behold yourself". They must open their eyes just for a brief instant to capture the image and then we walk on.

Like the poet Amergin we begin to see ourselves in all the wonders and mysteries of Nature. Often at this time I send people out to describe seven found wonders in the first person, beginning "I am". Then we sit in a circle and read them out in a round one at a time, creating a single piece of poetry in the style of Amergin.

Thus we gather the wonder of ourselves together and honour who we truly are.

Now as July comes to a close and the grain fattens in the fields and the fruit begins to swell on the trees we begin to gather too the goodness of the year, the fruits of our labours so far. We have followed the cycle through descent into reawakening and on to empowerment. We have dreamed, we have sown, we have tended. Now it is time to harvest.

First fruits

August begins with the fires of Lammas, honouring the earth as mother and celebrating the first fruits of the harvest. Originally known as Lughnasadh, a feast held for the sun god Lugh, it was renamed by the Anglo Saxon Christians. A loaf was traditionally baked with grain reaped at the very beginning of the harvest and this was offered at the mass. So the festival became known as Loaf mass or Lammas.

As we walk through the countryside at this time the first fruits are a harvest for the senses. The fields of wheat stand like golden platters upon Nature's table, abundant with grain swelling in the sunshine. In the orchard the fruit trees reveal their ripening treasures as cherries, pears, plums and apples push out shamelessly from among the leaves, swollen with colour, scent, promise and invitation, their whole purpose to seduce. In the woods the wild fruit is filling, the hazelnuts, acorns and beech nuts cluster like nesting creatures among the foliage while the ash and sycamore seeds hang like keys upon a gaoler's belt.

Away from the countryside it is easy to forget the harvest as our supermarkets provide us with what ever we want all year round. As the peak of the holiday season August often invites us to harvest the fruits of our labours in other ways as we head for the beaches and redden and ripen ourselves. But this event is more than just a gathering of food, this is the time when we are beginning to harvest the first fruits of our personal growth throughout the year however conscious or unconscious that has been.

First fruits can be sharp and bitter to the taste. The fullness of summer brings with it its own expectations and these can be hard to meet. The summer lands are supposed to be overflowing with milk and honey, a land of eternal youth and beauty. It is easy to find ourselves believing that everyone else is there except us. The holiday stretches on around us while we may struggle on beneath our dark and dismal clouds.

But Lammas is a time for gratitude, a time to thank the mother for her abundant gifts. Depending upon the mothering we received as children, gratitude may be a hard fruit to grow. If we were taught that life will rarely smile upon us then negativity will be the crop that we tend to harvest year after year and negativity spreads like a weed. Gratitude will not thrive in such conditions but if we work hard at growing it there it will slowly take over. Once it has taken hold it is the best of all cures for negativity because a grateful heart may be bothered by a negative mind but it will not be ruled by it.

So the first fruits give us an opportunity to cultivate gratitude. Gather some around you, a hazelnut in your pocket, a crab apple by your bed, an ash key slipped into your diary, a bunch of cherries hung from the rear view mirror of your car. Every time you see or touch them give thanks for what ever you can think of. Family, health, love, new opportunities, even the harsh lessons learned, there can be much that we take for granted that would devastate us if it was taken. The more we give thanks for what we have the more we invite life to bless us.

The dark harvest

The tree of harvest for the Celts here in the British Isles was the apple, a tree of love, abundance and healing. For the Celts on the continent it was the grape vine. Both trees produced sacred and intoxicating drinks.

The apple was one of the chieftain trees of Britain and its fruit was regarded as magical, a symbol of beauty and fruitfulness. In myth apples often speak to us of choice, consequence and destiny. The god Hermes gave Paris an apple and told him to award it to the most beautiful of the goddesses. He chose Aphrodite in return for the love of Helen of Sparta. The other goddesses, shunned and furious, lashed out at the city of Troy where Paris and Helen took refuge and the Trojan War began. In Genesis, it was Eve's choice to eat the apple from the tree of knowledge that led to their expulsion from the garden, the fall from innocence. In fairy tales also, apples often test us. Snow White ignored the advice of the dwarves and chose to accept the apple that poisoned her. In the Firebird a young prince set out on a quest to capture the bird that was stealing the golden apples from his father's tree. He was guided by a wolf, his teacher and pathfinder, yet time and time again he chose to ignore the wolf's advice and got himself into deeper and deeper trouble.

These stories suggest that on the path to wisdom and fulfillment there is usually a dark harvest first. Certainly in times of transition such as mid life or menopause, it is the dark and bitter fruit of our lives that we must face before we can come to a place of peace and acceptance within ourselves. Here in the dark harvest we learn about our mistakes, our frailties, our ego and the illusions that bewitch and betray it. Now in August as we begin to harvest the fruit of our practical and emotional endeavors throughout the year so far, it is often the dark harvest that we feel first.

The dark harvest is the gathering of the years shadow together under one wing to be felt again. Just as the wild vines of the forest wrap and tangle around all of the trees, binding all together, so the dark harvest embraces elements of all that we have passed through so far. We find ourselves revisiting emotional dead lands that we thought we had left behind. Even in the most hopeful transformation, as we emerge from our chrysalis and stretch our wings, we must grieve the loss of the world that we are leaving and those that sustained us there. This is the first harvest and the fires of Lammas arise to burn away the chaff and leave the good grain that will feed us and plant the fields of our future. In the shadow of the harvest is the beginning of decline. The sun nears the end of its yearly reign, the nights draw in and we stand with Lugh the sun god facing the underworld below the horizon. Having risen so far the fear of our own decline can find us here.

In the Irish myth of the battles of Magh Tuiredh the King of the Tuatha De Danann was so impressed by the talents of the young stranger Lugh that he abdicated in his favour, believing the young warrior to be better qualified to win the battle than he.

Lugh's grandfather was Balar of the evil eye and he led the Fomorians, the enemy. It had been prophesied that Balar would be killed by his grandson so he had imprisoned his daughter in a cave. But she was found, seduced and gave birth to triplets. Balar threw the children into the sea but one survived and this was Lugh.

Balar had an eye with a poisonous gaze that could slay a whole army. As soon as Lugh saw the great eye opening he cast a sling shot at it, driving the eye out the back of Balar's head, slaying Balar and casting its dreadful gaze upon the Fomorians instead. So Lugh won the battle.

As we falter under the weight of dark harvest and feel our decline again, so a wave of negativity can sweep over us like Balar's evil eye, threatening to end our quest just as we near its conclusion. We too must muster our masculine, just like Lugh of the long arm, and turn the raw power of the shadow upon itself.

It is important to honour the dark harvest before we can enjoy the light. Sometimes we find a tree that has a hollow at heads height within which we can place a candle. Then we gather totems or make images of our own dark harvest, our fears, our disappointments, our sorrows. Honouring these we offer up this bitter fruit and the feeling it evokes. Then we light the candle to represent the evil eye and standing at a distance we hurl our stones and our greater, angry truths until it is put out.

The weight of the world

Sometimes, to truly honour the dark harvest, we must feel the weight of it. Because it is a gathering of all the year's shadow it can weigh heavily upon us and leave us feeling downtrodden and wretched. It is hard to act when we feel like this. But the purpose of the weight is to provoke us sufficiently so that we might raise our indignation and cast it off. We can ritualize this, making a yoke by binding rocks to a branch, or rolling our totems of the dark harvest in a blanket. These can then be placed over or upon the shoulders and borne. If we are working in a group, others can add their weight to it, pulling it down from behind and beside us. Feeling the weight bearing down upon us, we consider who in our past placed it there and why and who has added to it for their own sake, until we are angry enough to throw it off.

Punching apples is another great way to raise and release the masculine. String some nice big apples up from a low branch so that they hang at head height. Now identify the things or the people that you need to get angry at. Name each apple as one of these, speak your truth to it and punch it as hard as you can. Apples are quite tough and a half hearted punch will probably hurt you more than it will the apple, which will just swing around the branch. But use your voice, find your power, and hit it with the full force of your fury and it will explode in the most dramatic and satisfying way.

Carved on a hillside in Dorset is a huge chalk giant, erect and defiant and wielding a great club above his head. Believed to be either an image of Lugh or Heracles, this god man stands as a totem of power and fertility, a shining solar deity defending the harvest from the forces of decline and despair. It was Lugh who sent the sons of Tuirenn to find for him the magical apples that grew in the Garden of light. It was Heracles who shot Ladon the serpent and took the weight of the sky upon his shoulders so that Atlas could steal the apples of immortality from the garden of the

146

Hesperides. Just as Lugh had overcome the evil eye of his grandfather, so Heracles, by his labours, overcame the madness that had made him kill his own family. We too, by our labours, can drive back the shadows and begin to reap the harvest that is our due. We too can reach for the apples.

In druidic lore the apple orchards of paradise were known as the Isles of the Blessed and there on the tree of knowledge grew three sacred apples, guarded by a serpent who was a personification of the goddess Ceriddwen, the crone. The garden, the apple, the serpent. Again and again we find these motifs clustered together in myths from different corners of the world. When Eve, the feminine incarnate, reached for the forbidden fruit she began a process that led us all from the place of innocence, through a vale of shadows and on, to a deeper, richer understanding of self, of our frailties, our temptations and our God given power to overcome.

Prophecy

As the harvest comes into its fullness, the land becomes smothered and overgrown as that which is not cut back or gathered rejoices in its wildness. Woodland pathways are lost beneath the bracken, while nettles and brambles invade the clearings and the forest vines choke and strangle the trees. Throughout the countryside there is a sense of abandonment, of life running amok and going to seed.

In this seed is the first hint of what is to come. So far is it from fruition that it appears to us now as just a fleeting and intangible intuition, as prophecy. The Queen of Faerie gave apples to those who sought the gift of prophecy and in the thirteenth century Thomas of Ercledoune is said to have visited her in the land of Faerie and received this gift. Merlin is said to have carried around with him a magical orchard that he could manifest at will. The trees here produced apples that held the secrets of the earth and the understanding of the movements of the planets. To eat these apples would bring great wisdom and the knowledge of what is to come.

The vine too was associated with prophecy and was sacred to Dionysius, the god of wine, drama and altered states. He personified abandonment and wildness and his followers were the satyrs, part man, part goat, who were addicted to wine, revelry and lust, and the maenads, women driven to such madness by his worship that they would rip apart any man who strayed into their rituals. Dionysius was the son of Semele, a mortal woman who was seduced by Zeus. Hera, out of jealousy, disguised herself as an old woman and persuaded Semele to ask her lover to show himself in his full glory. Zeus reluctantly agreed and Semele was burned to a cinder by the raw incandescence of the god. But Zeus saved the child Dionysius from the ashes and stitched him into his own thigh.

So Dionysius was born from the death of his own mother, and now as we harvest the body of the mother his spirit is born again around and within us. For we harvest not only the staple crops that we planted and tended, such as work, relationship and lifestyle, but also the wild fruit that grew of its own accord in the spaces that we did not attend to. This is the fruit of the feminine, our creativity, our passion, our wild and dancing spirit.

The apple teaches us much about our relationship with wildness. An orchard is a beautiful place, an oasis of vibrant colour, peace and fertility. It celebrates wildness, yet if it becomes too wild it fails. If the apple trees are not cut back every year they fruit less and less until they become too heavy and are blown over in the wind. So it is with us. Wildness becomes us, it liberates and enriches us but if we do not attend to ourselves and our personal process we may slip into old and habitual patterns, parental legacies and dysfunctional coping mechanisms. Paradoxically we need to turn the wild energy of Dionysius upon itself, to cut down the wild weeds that would stifle us and free the child within.

For it is the child, the new seed, that is left when the mother is cut down. In the orchard the child is reborn year after year, as long as the trees are tended.

One of the names for Dionysius was Lusios, meaning releaser, for his cult involved ecstatic release brought on by dance, music and wine. The earliest theatre evolved from these rituals but soon became a media for storytelling. Drama provided the means to bring mythology to life, an infinite storeroom in which the harvest of old tales and sacred stories could be kept safe and fresh to feed the imagination of the people. But within this storeroom, this collective unconscious, there was much mixing and tangling as tales interwove and fermented together, so the wine that was made from these fruits changed with time and location. This is a Dionysian quality for he was a changeling, a master of illusion. When he was captured by pirates the knots that they tied to bind him kept untying of their own accord, then wine flowed around the ship and vines grew from the mast. Finally he became a lion and the pirates leapt into the sea to escape him, where they were turned into dolphins.

As we awaken the masculine to shake off the dark harvest it is the lion within ourselves that roars and the ties that bind us that dissolve in consequence. We too can enact our dramas, making and performing stories from random things found in nature and then scrutinizing these tales in retrospect for the prophecies that they hold. Or we can make masks of bark and leaf and berry, of woven stalks, of moss and feathers and shells. Then we can tell our life's tales, their twists and their turns, their mysteries, synchronicities and lessons. Once we wove masks from willow and decorated them with grass and reed and flowers. Each mask was the face of the character we become when the dark harvest overwhelms us. Faces of fear, despair, negativity, confusion and grief. One by one we put on our masks and allowed Lusios to release the dark spirit within us, becoming our own bitter shadow. Then when its force was spent, we removed the mask, destroyed it and set ourselves free.

For many years I worked with people who had profound and complex disabilities. Hardly anyone could talk and most had very limited mobility and yet we made up the most extraordinary stories together. Working in the garden we would collect up leaves, flowers, fir cones, feathers, stones and other such treasures and take them around the group. As an item was chosen and played with we would improvise the story accordingly. As group members interacted with each other we would improvise still, inspired by the sounds that people made, the things that they did and the ways that they moved. The stories held a freedom of metaphor that I have never encountered before or since where magical and completely unexpected things just happened as a matter of course. As storyteller my task was to recount it, make some sense of it and round it off at the end. As therapist my task was to make sure that everyone was involved, that all responses were honoured and that opportunities for growth and development were taken. But as participant my task was just to wonder. Each story was unique and was uniquely the property of the group that created it. Many contained moments of uncanny synchronicity and profound healing. Some were so amazing that they have stayed with me to this day.

Some we turned into performance. Building huge carnival characters and creatures, many on wheelchairs, and performing in the dark using the torches fixed within them, we created a mysterious and dreamlike form of outdoor theatre in which gods and goddesses walked the earth, and in which people with severe disabilities could be involved without the emphasis being placed upon their special needs. We called this Dreamtime theatre and for many years we use this art form to lead large community arts events, celebrations and rituals. Because everything required audience participation anyone and everyone, regardless of needs or skills, could be involved either as a performer or as a participant. Many of the stories that we told had prophetic qualities. One in particular that continues to guide me was a performance involving the characters carved on a totem pole by the visiting native Canadians with whom we had held hands around the ancient yew. The story was about Ilchinik the whaler. Ilchinik did not go out and hunt the whales as other whalers would. Instead he would prepare himself ritually and inwardly and then the whales would come to him. This story has taught me so much about the nature of harvest and in many ways it is definitive of environmental arts therapy.

So Dionysius offers us a wildness of metaphor where anything can become anything else and this is the gift of the storyteller. He offers freedom from the restraints of our beliefs; he blows away the shrouds of illusion like so much thistledown and lets us see that anything is possible. The knots that bind us suddenly untie.

This in itself can be unsettling as in the harvesting of the fruit we must let go of that into which we have invested so much love and effort. But in doing so we rediscover the clear ground beneath and find ourselves standing on a new threshold with a handful of seeds and an open view.

In the stories that we share and the dramas of our lives we honour this wild harvest, this gathering of the seemingly unconnected bound together by a greater mystery. Sometimes there is little to cling to but the synchronicity that runs like a thin golden thread through the chaos, like a vine seeking the light.

The light that we seek shines always in the orchard that we carry within ourselves, like Merlin, spending a lifetime learning how to manifest it. Paradise, a Persian word, means orchard. Here in the Eden within, where the sun shines always through the green and leafy boughs, we find the apple that shines brightest, the love of self. The apple was the symbol of Aphrodite, goddess of love, and these apples are all those things in life that nourish, celebrate and enrich us. As we grow they grow within and around us. It is up to us to pick them.

Choosing life

Prince Ivan in the Russian tale of the Firebird was led by the wolf to another king's palace where the firebird was kept. "Take the bird" said the wolf "but on no account touch the golden cage in which it sits" Ivan removed the bird but then, unable to resist the beautiful cage, decided to take that too. An alarm set the guards upon him and he was taken to the king. As punishment he was sent to another kingdom to steal a horse with a golden mane. Again the wolf advised him. "Take the horse" he said "but do not touch the golden bridle that hangs beside him." Again Ivan is tempted and again he is caught. This time as punishment he is sent to carry off Princess Vasilisa the fair from her father's home. But as soon as the young people meet they fall in love and the wolf helps Ivan win the princess for himself.

This story tells us much about choice and its consequences. When we are tempted again and again by life's trappings it is decline and decay that we are choosing because these things are material, transient and passing. These golden trappings serve only to trap life, to restrain and cage it and they represent the fearful need to cling to and control that which is inherently flowing and changeable. Because they only sustain us for a while the grasping becomes addictive and we are never truly satisfied. So we are condemned to go on quest after quest, seeking greater and more elusive treasures, stealing the riches from the world yet harvesting only disappointment. But when we choose life it is beauty and abundance that we are choosing because life is eternal, creating itself out of itself for ever. Life is wild and spontaneous, passionate and vital. Reaching only for those things that truly nourish, sustain and enliven us, we harvest life itself. Then we too are reunited with the feminine and give life back to the world.

This choice is presented to us every moment of our lives. Do we fill the day doing the jobs that need doing or do we go for a swim in the river? Do we make those important telephone calls or do we play with the children in the woods? Do we spend the afternoon shopping or do we plant trees on the meadow? Choosing life means living simply, enjoying simple pleasures. There is a guiding voice within each of us that, just like Ivan's wolf, knows exactly what we need and what we don't. We just have to take time to listen.

This choice has global consequences too. It is the relentless quest for the trappings that leads us to plunder and pollute our world. Yet the real pleasures in life such as love, reverence, friendship, sharing, and celebration take nothing from the planet. They give life back to itself and without them all the trappings in the world are meaningless.

In Russian fairy tales parents are often referred to as little mother and little father, even when they are royal. This term is not meant to diminish them but to honour their humanity, to differentiate them from the greater mother, Nature, and the greater father, God. We can spend a lifetime learning to make this differentiation, because when we are young our parents carry the mantel of the archetypal upon their shoulders and consequently their influence upon us is vast. Even if they are absent or impotent, the lessons that they teach us about absence and impotence infuse every part of our being. Only as we grow and work through the issues that they bequeath upon us do we begin to really see their littleness in the order of things. They are the instruments of life's often harsh but always enriching lessons, and are themselves of course only human.

This is often the work of midlife, a time of great harvesting for all of us. The change that midlife can bring can be so profound that by the time we reach fifty we are not the same person that we were ten years before. Yet because our culture does not honour the cycles of the feminine our language has no words for what we become. The terms child, adult and elder do not encompass this dramatic transformation which, when we do our inner work, overwhelms us midway and which is so vital that if we do not embrace it, we will almost certainly become ill. Perhaps we could say that when we are young we are children so when we are young adults we are elder children. Likewise when we are old we are elders so when we are past midlife we are child elders. For it is the robe of the elder that we begin making for ourselves at midlife, and in doing so we release our own parents to be little again.

Often midlife requires us to let go of our own children as well. As the child becomes an adult and begins to pull away there is much grief and much ambivalence. We grieve the loss of the child that we loved. We cling to that child because we have invested so much of our own inner child's needs within it. Now as it pulls away, as it must, we may feel cheated, betrayed and abandoned. Old feelings of rejection and abandonment that have their source in our own childhood can be triggered again. Yet at the same time we want and need them to go. We want to pull away too, to rediscover our own freedom and begin to nourish the neglected child within, yet something tells us that we are still needed. To let go and yet still be there is a great challenge in the face of all the sadness and anger that can be evoked at this time. Working through this ambivalence consciously and honestly with a reluctant teenager is hard for any parent.

When we go into therapy the therapist takes on a parental role but with much clearer boundaries than that which we may have encountered before. The work of the parent in this context has many of the attributes of the masculine, to think, to interpret, to keep safe, to watch the time, to come up with ideas, to explain and to direct. The therapist becomes all mind, and heart is put to one side. That is not to say that they are unfeeling, quite the opposite, but the feelings of the therapist act as an inner compass and barometer for the therapist and are rarely openly shared. This role is taken on by the therapist so that as the client we are left with nothing to do but feel. Perhaps for the first time we are allowed to enter fully into our feminine knowing that someone else is holding the space. It can be a difficult descent. But it can also be one of the most beautiful and rewarding journeys that we ever make.

However harvesting the fruit of this journey often means completing it. Leaving therapy we may feel that never again will we find that precious space where we felt so honoured. But here once again we are given the opportunity that comes with harvest, to exchange the little parent for the greater one.

Because the little parent is external our relationship with them is based around dependency, whether they are mother, father, spouse or therapist. But the greater parent is within. We may see the bounteous earth stretching out around us but it is inside our hearts that we feel the love of the great mother. We may see the dark sky filling with stars above us but it is inside our minds that we awaken to the will of the great father. When we cultivate a relationship with these parents, it is self sufficiency that we harvest.

So when we go alone into Nature we can seek to be both therapist and client to ourselves. As therapist I keep myself safe, I am aware of the passage of time, I watch for clues to my process, I interpret metaphor, I follow the tracks of feeling, I do not judge myself, I let myself be, I take myself to the place of greatest resistance, I hold myself, I witness myself and I honour myself.

As client I seek only to feel, I cry, I rage, I express my fears, my guilt and my shame, I meet hope, I find love, joy and reverence within myself, I wonder, I laugh, I find peace.

I choose life.

Apple men and corn dollies

At harvest time the growing year has come full cycle and in traditional communities the bringing in of the fruit, grain and vegetables is a cause for great celebration. Many rituals mark the completion of the harvest. Traditionally the last apple is left on the tree for the apple man, the wise old spirit of the apple tree who ensures future harvests. We too can make apple men, joining apples together by pushing a stick into one and then pushing the second apple onto it. We can give them arms and legs, faces and clothes. We can make apple animals too. Children especially enjoy this and having made their characters will happily make their homes and communities as well.

In pre Christian Europe it was common for the reaper who cut the last sheaf of the cereal crop to offer his blood in return. Some believed that whoever cut the last sheaf killed the corn spirit and would have bad luck, so all the reapers would throw their sickles together.

This folklore speaks to us of great ambivalence, of celebration and of loss as the mother is slain and her body harvested. Many communities honoured this by using the last sheaf to make a corn dolly. In the north of England she was called a kirn doll and she was carried to the harvest supper. In Pembrokeshire she was the hag. In Poland she was called Baba, or old woman, and would be made by two girls who delivered her to the farmer with a garland. These images of the feminine would be kept throughout the winter as a safe lodging for the spirit of the field and in the spring the grain of this sheaf would be sown along with the rest of the stored seed.

The corn dolly is an image of Demeter, the grain mother, also known as Ceres. As the sister of Zeus she was an archetype of Mother Earth. She protected the soil and its bounty and the Eleusinian mysteries, the most famous and widely celebrated mystery cult in the ancient world, revolved around her.

Demeter is a symbol of fertility, motherhood and abundance but her shadow is dependence and the fear evoked by it. When hunting and gathering was replaced by subsistence agriculture the people's trust in Nature to provide for their means was replaced by a reliance on the annual harvest, and its failure meant famine. The fear of this motivates communities to replace the natural replenishing force of Nature with their own labour in an attempt to guarantee enough for all and this creates a work ethic that sacrifices the self for the sake of the community. Even though few of us still live in farming communities this work ethic still weighs heavily upon us. We can still be bound by fear, not necessarily of starvation, but of failure, losing our homes, our jobs, our status. This can harness us to work that does not nourish our true and creative selves. Year after year we may harvest the fruit of this lifestyle yet even though our crops may look abundant to others the central core of our being can become starved and depleted.

If you cut an apple in half across its middle, the core appears as a five pointed star, the symbol of Aphrodite, goddess of love. It is this cradle of love at the very core of ourselves that seeks to protect and cherish the seeds of all that we would become, if we let it, just as Demeter sought to protect her daughter when she was stolen by Hades. Demeter's daughter was called Kore, or Persephone. When she was abducted and taken down to the underworld Demeter mourned the loss of her child and withheld the grain from the world. So it is with us if we sacrifice the child within, our all pervading sorrow will drain the goodness from our lives.

As Demeter wandered the world looking for her child she was taken into the service of King Celeus to act as attendant for his wife Mataneira. The queen asked Demeter to nurse her son Demophoon. Every night the goddess secretly fed the boy on ambrosia and laid him on the fire to burn away his mortality. Mataneira discovered this and in her horror she snatched the child from the fire. Demeter revealed her true self and angrily told the mother that she had cost Demophoon his immortality.

So it is that the fearfulness of the mother, the restrictions and familiar patterns and constraints of old ways, keeps our inner child from its divine and boundless self. But in harvest, as the mother is slain, comes a new opportunity. With the cutting down of the old year comes a real sense that anything is possible. We leave behind the little mother with her limited vision and enter into a fuller relationship with the greater mother, with whom our opportunities are boundless. With the gathering of seed we hold the child once again in our hand and awaken to the potential for a way of life that honours and nourishes that pure and creative self within.

So usually at this time we make corn dollies. There are traditional ways of making these but we usually just improvise using whatever long grasses, leaves and flowers we can harvest at the time. Consequently the variety of little human figures that emerge is always entrancing. Grassy little effigies clad in thistle and dock leaf, with flowers in their hair, rosehips and blackberries clutched in their arms, bejeweled with snail shells and hazelnuts, seated on a mossy stump, perched in a cherry tree astraddle a branch or standing upright by the waters edge, their feet in the mud. We visit and honour each other's dolls and share our feelings about all that we have harvested. Then, into their little bodies we push apple seeds to name and affirm the things that we wish to grow in the next cycle of our lives.

Once I gave a group of men a scythe and asked them to cut the path to their dreams through the long grass, flowers and thistles on a hillside. The scythe was rather blunt and they had to really work at it. Then they made corn dollies out of all that they had cropped. Sitting on that dark hillside under the stars watching these strong and passionate men making dolls by torchlight is a memory that will always stay with me.

The pendulum of the year that swings incessantly back and forth between masculine and feminine begins to turn again. Summer is ending. The urgent outward push of the masculine that has propelled us this far beyond the summer solstice and led us to the place of harvest can maintain its impetus no longer and we tip back inwards again. The descent begins. The end of the cycle is approaching but the work is not yet complete.

For something is waiting in the shadows.

Chapter 11 September

The labyrinth

September comes and the nights creep in, a coolness settles around and within us and there is a sense of turning. The solar energy of the masculine is losing its power and recoiling and we begin now to spiral inward once again. The hedgerows become laden with dark fruit, blackberries, sloes and elderberries. This is a return to the feminine and her shadowy riches.

Even before the leaves start yellowing we know that autumn is here. We feel the change of direction within ourselves, a desire to return like the snail into the spiral of our being. The sun may still be shining but it is a little lower in the sky now and it picks out the cobwebs in the hedgerows and sets them ablaze in the morning when the dewdrops held upon them sparkle like strings of diamonds. The days can be soft, hazy and warm but the nights are growing colder. The unharvested fruit and grain is falling by itself now, mouldering in the long grass, attracting mice, squirrels and birds. There is a sense of gathering for there is both bounty now and hard times ahead. Life is beginning to pull inwards, collapsing its systems, folding its wings about itself, taking stock, settling down and preparing for the endings to come.

One of the plants that the Celts associated with this time was the ivy. They considered the ivy the strongest of trees because it can choke and kill anything it grows on, even the great oak. It can block a path or pull down a wall and when we meet a huge and ancient ivy we do not just meet the plant, with its thick and serpentine sinews, but we confront also that which is hidden within. Something suffocated, ruined and forgotten. So ivy draws us inwards, into the labyrinth of our being, to meet that which still blocks our path to freedom. As the cycle of the year nears its end it is often here that we meet the aspect of our self that we keep most hidden from ourselves and others. As we return from the summerlands it awaits us.

The Greek god Zeus desired the princess Europa and disguising himself as a white bull he carried her over the sea to Crete and ravished her. She bore him three sons: Minos, Rhadamanthys and Sarpedon, all of whom were adopted by the Cretan king Asterios when he found and married their mother. When they grew up Minos claimed the throne and asked for a sign from Poseidon to show that his claim was favoured by the gods. Poseidon sent a magnificent white bull from the sea on the understanding that Minos sacrifice it directly back to him, but Minos coveted the bull for his own herd and he sacrificed the second best instead. Poseidon was angered and he punished Minos by causing his wife Pasiphae to fall in love with the bull.

Pasiphae longed for union with the bull and persuaded the craftsman Daedelus to construct a wooden cow for her to conceal herself in. The union was consummated and Pasiphae gave birth to the Minotaur, half man, half bull. To hide their shame Minos told Daedelus to build an elaborate labyrinth within which to imprison the monstrous child, and each year nine boys and nine girls were sent from Athens as food for the beast. Then one year Theseus the son of the king of Athens asked to be sent as one of the sacrifices. With the help of Ariadne, king Minos' daughter, who gave him a golden thread that allowed him to find his way back through the labyrinth, Theseus found and slew the Minotaur.

Theseus and the Minotaur are twin aspects of the same self. One golden, privileged and heroic, the other wounded, neglected and monstrous. Each of us has a Minotaur of sorts, a dark twin that is imprisoned within, yet whose demands we must satisfy with sacrifice. When Theseus confronted and overcame the beast he reintegrated the whole. Indeed on his return journey he abandoned Ariadne, who had loved and aided him, on the island of Naxos and as he approached Athens he neglected to take down the black sail of death as he had promised his father Aegeus. When the king saw the sail he thought his son dead and cast himself off the cliff into the sea, henceforth known as the Aegean. So Theseus becomes both hero and monster.

We too build our labyrinths at this time. We make them out of branches in the woods or mark their winding paths with stones and ridges of sand on the beach. We cut their passageways through old bracken or find them already intact, made by badgers and deer in the undergrowth. All of these are large enough to walk into but we can make little ones too, spirals of moss coiling ever inwards on an old stump, little walkways on the riverbank framed by twig fences stuck in the mud, twists of ivy pinned with thorns to the forest floor.

We visualize our journeys here, and make these journeys by foot into the greater labyrinths and by fingertip into the lesser. As we stand at the entrance we describe what we see and feel. As we enter and journey within we describe what we find and encounter. If we wish to make the journey in darkness we can close our eyes and ask someone else to guide us. At each junction they ask us to choose which way to go. So we venture inwards, into the secret chambers of ourselves and meet whoever or whatever is there to be met.

It is the spirit of Theseus, the heroic masculine, which we summon now, as we descend once again into the labyrinth within to meet the shadows that await us there. Ariadne's golden thread is like the silk of the spider and it leads us in spirals to the centre of our web, where waits something fearful, grown fat on all that we have sacrificed to it. This is the last block in the cycle of the year, the meeting with the dark twin cloaked still in the shadows of our childhood.

Ivy calls us now into this reunion. To spiral down and meet the one we fear most. To reclaim the disowned self and heal that which was broken.

The feminine is by its nature a very fragile thing so a child can be easily broken. All our little souls are born with great hopes. The hope that we will be loved, held, heard, nurtured, allowed to thrive, allowed to be ourselves, allowed to grow without judgement, condemnation or shame. When these expectations are not met there comes a time in our childhood when hope cannot sustain us any longer and something breaks. We will always remember this time, the time that I sat on the stairs and wept, the time that I ran and hid in the woods, the time that I stood in the window and thought about jumping. They may seem like small insignificant memories now but we will never forget them, even though the rest of our childhood may be lost in a fog of forgetfulness, and when we explore them in therapy we find that they hold great feeling. For this was the point when something within us got left behind. Something wronged, something angry, something that could find no voice in childhood. In order just to carry on we bundled up this shadow and hid it in the dank and dusty cupboards of our heart. Or we left it on the stairway, up the tree or trembling at the window sill and we walked away. Now so many years later we must return to these places and find it again.

But this can be a daunting task because while we have been growing and changing, the shadow has too. Keep a wounded child in the dark long enough and it will become a Minotaur. Because it resides within us, because it is part of us, we can never escape from its needs. Its hunger can be warped and dreadful. We may try with the best intentions to soldier on, to be the heroic masculine, an adult of honour, valour and integrity. But the beast will demand its sacrifices anyway and we will be compelled to feed it. So the dark corner of the heart becomes a den of self perpetuating shame and remorse. Only by entering this place and reconciling ourselves with the one we find within can we become whole.

Spiders and their prey

When I was a little boy I had an obsession with woodlice. I would make them little mossy islands in trays of water. I would build them little mazes out of slate and watch them find their way out. I learned that they had negative phototaxis, which means that they are compelled to seek the dark. I loved to watch them give birth as their swollen yellow tummies dissolved into a mass of tiny seething babies. But also, I am rather ashamed to remember, I inflicted some dreadful punishments upon them. One of these was the ant jar, an awful fate for any small insect. But possibly the death sentence I relished most was popping them into a spider's web and watching the spider come. There was something gladiatorial about this, or perhaps Christians and lions, as the woodlouse stood little chance despite its armour. If it was clever it stayed very, very still. But woodlice are rarely clever.

When we meet old and dense ivy we encounter a world of shadows and cobwebs, and ivy clad buildings are notoriously spider infested. In September the hedgerows too are full of cobwebs, each with a spider at the centre, fattened by a summer of flies. Little traps and snares are woven everywhere, glinting in the low autumn sun, waiting for prey.

When we meet our ivy block we rarely see it coming but suddenly find ourselves held fast, like a fly in the web. It feels impenetrable and it can bring with it a great sense of helplessness. The more we struggle the more we call the beast that waits at the centre of the spiral towards us.

Arachne was a princess who was so skilled in the art of weaving that the goddess Athene, patron of all the arts of women, could not compete with her. She tried to find fault in a beautiful illustrated cloth that Arachne had woven but when she could not she tore it up in a rage. On hearing this Arachne hung herself from a rafter for fear of the goddess. Athene found her and turned her into a spider, the creature that the goddess hated most, and Arachne ran up her thread and hid.

160

Athene was the most powerful goddess in the Greek pantheon but having been born from a wound in the skull of Zeus after he had devoured her mother; she was a goddess of the head rather than the heart and was famed for her wisdom, teaching and military tactics. Here is a rich cultural metaphor, the patriarchal masculine had swallowed up the feminine and given birth to a goddess that could only be valued in male terms. So she remained a virgin and repulsed all sexual advances including an attempted rape by the god Hephaestus. Her dislike of spiders is interesting because the spiders we encounter wandering around our homes are invariably male, as the females stay in the webs, and they often appear as metaphors for dark and invasive masculine energy.

When Athene found a young girl called Medusa lying with the god Poseidon in one of her temples she was so furious that she turned her into a gorgon, a winged monster with snakes for hair, whose gaze could turn men into stone. Once again the innocent feminine was punished, due to the jealousy of a goddess and the lust of a god. So it is that unconscious and dysfunctional parenting creates monsters in the hearts of children that then remain disowned and hidden into adulthood.

A child can no more stand up to the unconscious wounding by their parents than Medusa could have stood up to the god and goddess that abused her. So the separation of the child into the outwardly obedient and the inwardly monstrous comes from a place of learned helplessness. It is this helplessness that can sweep over us now as we find ourselves caught once again in the web of our own wounding. It is our own dark and neglected self that comes to meet us then.

Athene assisted the hero Perseus in his quest to slay Medusa by giving him a shield so polished that it could be used as a mirror. So Perseus, the heroic masculine, confronted and beheaded the gorgon without looking directly at her. So it is in therapy that we can meet and reintegrate the shadow using metaphor to reflect and contain its power and retain a safe therapeutic distance. Perseus gave the head of Medusa to Athene who wore it on her breastplate to petrify her enemies. So the cold goddess finally honoured the power of the dark feminine, wearing it upon her heart.

Caught in the web of the wounded self we too must call upon our heroic masculine to face the monster. After the gorgon is slain Perseus rescued Andromeda just as Theseus carried off Ariadne after slaying the Minotaur. Both liberate a new feminine from the old web.

So this is a good time to make spider's webs. Find a crook in a tree between branches and mark out the boundaries of your web with soft wool that will easily break down with time. Now make lines of wool leading from the outside of the web to its centre, like the spokes of a bicycle. Then starting from the centre spiral outward, looping the wool around each spoke as you go. It takes a little practice to get the tension right, but with time you can end up with the most magnificent giant webs. Often we make images of ourselves within them, the fly tightly bound in silk like a deathly papoose, the spider fat and hungry and waiting to pounce, the wasp fighting for its life, sting against bite, the sacrificed woodlouse abandoned to its fate.

In Native America, a culture that honoured the feminine, the spider is said to have woven a web that created the Earth and the first human beings were made by spider woman. Here the feminine sits where it belongs, at the feeling, manifesting centre of the web, weaving its reality around it. Here the goddess does not fear spiders, she is one, and she celebrates her creativity, her sexuality and her location at the heart of all things.

The heart of all things

I have heard it said that the heart of a woman is her cervix. This suggests that the feminine is at heart a doorway through which life comes. The power of the feminine is its innate ability to create and manifest, bringing into reality the dreams and fantasies of the inner world. This is a boundless power and it can stand at odds with the power of the masculine which seeks to understand, shape and control all that exists, in the same way that magic stands at odds with science. So the masculine may be compelled to ridicule, disempower or condemn the feminine. This has long been a feature of our history, from the burning of witches to the oppression of women, to the shaming and breaking of our children's wild and magical spirits by unconscious parenting and cold and academic institutions. But it is all born of fear.

When my wife was pregnant with our daughter she tested positive for toxoplasmosis, a condition that can blind the child. In great shock and grief we went to Cornwall for a week with my son. We arrived at a café and were greeted by a beautiful white cat that then slipped away out of a window. We spent the week making art on the beaches and cliff tops to express and honour our fears. We met fear too, convinced that we had walked into a nest of adders we were paralyzed until slowly we realized it was all just fear. Every where we went we saw dragonflies, even on the jewellery of people that we met. Dragonflies are symbols of illusion and we began to suspect that our fears were no more than this. At last we found ourselves at St Michael's mount standing before a statue of St Michael overcoming the devil. It was from here that my wife made the call that informed us that further tests suggested that all might be well. We decided to trust. On the way home we stopped at the café again and the white cat reappeared at the window and came and loved us. We asked its name and we were told that it was Maya, also meaning illusion. Our daughter was born healthy and beautiful. We called her Maya.

Michaelmass, the feast of the archangel Michael, falls near the end of September. This image of the higher self overcoming fear is a powerful totem for our times but it is interesting that the devil is often portrayed as a serpent or dragon, ancient symbols of the feminine. It suggests that the struggle between the rational and controlling power of the masculine and the wild and magical power of the feminine is archetypal and therefore inherently at the heart of all things. The masculine seeks to tame and know all, the feminine is wild and unknowable and so it inspires fear. So the cervix clamps shut, the doorway is closed and what promises to be the pathway to our dreams becomes the ivy block. As our technology seeks to reconcile itself with climate change this is the block that we face. It seems insurmountable and it overwhelms us with fear. But the purpose of the ivy block is not to stop us but to test us.

As the autumn equinox calls the great stags out to bellow and fight we too are invited to reclaim the wild bull power of the dark twin and blast our way through the walls that imprison us. In the forest we build great barriers of wood, bramble and thorn, on the beaches we shoulder huge stones into walls that keep us from the surge and crash of the waves. We stoke up our fire, rage through the walls and run released beneath the trees, or into the ice cold September Sea. So the conscious intention of the masculine and the wild and passionate spirit of the feminine are reunited. Michael puts on the dragon skin, roars and breathes fire.

The voice of judgement

All around us the natural systems that have sustained us are now beginning to fail as the earth begins to draw its life giving fluids back into itself and the heat of the sun lessens. So our own failings and the judging voices that condemn them often come to our attention here. This is not surprising as it was the voice of judgement that first sentenced the shadow to exile. The voice of judgement may say many things. You are failing. You are weak. You are wrong. You are a fool to believe that which you believe in. You are wicked. You will never get it right. You are ugly. You will never succeed. You are useless. Whatever the voice says, the message is always the same: you are not good enough as you are. This message, once ingrained into our psyche will taint everything we do and everything we are. It will sell us short in every opportunity for love, happiness and freedom that comes our way. What is more, if we do not address it, we will almost certainly pass it on to our children.

It can be useful to make an image of judgement, a huge malevolent face carved into the sandy cliff, a great pointing hand made from branches in the wood, the rotten pedestal of an old tree stump upon which judgement can stand and rant. Usually these images are huge as that is how judgement feels, especially to a child, the child that we were and the child within. Judgement usually comes from a place of fear, self doubt and fragility, for only when we are unsure of ourselves do we use the voice of judgement upon others to make ourselves feel better. This is self perpetuating because when we judge our children they integrate the voice of judgement and continue to judge themselves into adulthood. Then because of the fear, self doubt and fragility that this creates, they judge their own children in the same way. So the legacy continues.

Another reason that judgement is passed on from generation to generation is that regardless of whatever our masculine strives for, be it wealth, status, power or security, all our feminine yearns for is freedom, happiness and love. Children, being born from the feminine, know this inherently and left to their own devices will seek nothing else. It is hard for us as adults, often so worn and jaded, having sacrificed so much of ourselves for work, security, responsibility and life style to then allow these free and passionate spirits to be. It is hard not to be jealous and resentful. It is far easier to start judging as we were judged, to try and mould them into the same shape as ourselves.

But the dark twin within ourselves will hate us for this. It is this rage that often emerges at this time, and we have to be careful not to use it against our children simply because they are next in the pecking order. If we wish to end the legacy then we must turn this power back upon judgement itself. We need to identify the voice of judgement, as a parent or a sibling or whoever, and rage against it. This may involve finding and removing a token of love and fragility from the heart of judgement first for as children we would have sensed this in the other and it will still stand in the way of our anger. But once it is removed it is only judgement

164

that we face with all of its bitter implications to our freedom, happiness and love. It is the voice of judgement both in ourselves and in others and we can turn the full fury of the shadow within us upon it. So the dark and awesome power within that we had feared and sacrificed to is suddenly released as a force for good, wiping the smear of judgement from the face of our lives.

The serpent and the eagle

By the end of September the leaves upon the trees are yellowing and starting to fall. All of the year's growth and the energy that has been invested in it are coming to an end. In preparation for a new cycle of growth the trees begin to let go of the old. So this is a time of release.

We too will probably have walked our labyrinth and met our blocks by now. Carl Jung describes the labyrinth as a matriarchal system, a place of confusion, secrets and hidden feelings. It is the old way of the repressed feminine, the legacy of queen Pacifae and her bull lover. A place where shame is hidden and roams the shadows waiting to be freed. When we tire of the sacrifice it demands of us, then our masculine can cut through these secrets like a knife. Our anger empowers us and our truth is our weapon.

When we find the monster child, the part of us that was locked away and reviled, and bring it out into the sun, everything changes. Suddenly we see our ivy in a new light. Instead of choking the tree, suffocating the ruin, blocking the path, we see its potential for freedom. Nothing stands in its way. It crawls across the forest floor and climbs over everything. It becomes a metaphor for our release.

In the Babylonian story of Etana, the king sought immortality. He went to the fire god Shamash who told him that he must fly up to heaven and talk to the goddess Ishtar. Etana went in search of an eagle great enough to carry him there and he found it imprisoned in the den of a giant serpent. Etana killed the snake and freed the eagle. Leaping on to its back he flew up to Heaven where Ishtar gave him the plant of rebirth.

So it can be for us at this time, as we emerge from the serpents den, the place of the dark feminine, we find an eagle's back awaiting us and its wings at our service. Often this sense of freedom comes just from a sudden change of perception, a shifting of the inner block that created the illusion of imprisonment. Suddenly we find that the brick wall was a doorway all along. From the eagle's back we see the whole world is open to us. In the cycle of our life, this is an experience that many describe as they move beyond the menopause and approach old age.

It is in this ascent that freedom is found. When Athene turned Arachne into a spider, she scuttled up her thread and hid in the rafters. Released at last from the affairs of gods and men, she was free. When in the therapeutic process we descend into feeling, honour and release it, we then make this ascent. Back up into the higher, wiser self, a place of knowing, peace and freedom. The more often we follow this cycle the easier it becomes to find this higher space within ourselves. Paradoxically it is only by frequent forays into the basement that we learn to live upstairs.

When we recognize the feeling, feminine self as our Holy Grail and make the seeking of it our life's quest, we find ourselves abiding more and more in this higher realm that some might call Heaven, where we can consciously manifest our dreams. But being humans not angels we can only abide here if we are willing to descend as we need to, as the cycle of the year demands. The serpent and the eagle are two sides of the same coin and we cannot have one without the other.

From the higher vantage point we look down upon our trials and tribulations and see that just like the myths and fairytales that guide and inspire us, our lives are just stories. Stories with beginnings and endings, unexpected twists, messages and meanings. Stories rich in synchronicity, metaphor and magic. Stories with lessons to share and inspire. Stories that stand upon the shoulders of other stories just as the tale of Theseus stood upon that of Minos. Stories that mix and weave like the threads of Arachne's cloth.

Working in a group it is good to weave our storylines together in this way. Each of us makes a line on the ground that illustrates our life so far. This can be done with flour or with found objects and materials. We need to work this out as a group for the intention is for each line to cross or travel alongside another according to the relationship that we have had with that person. So if we met briefly when we were young there is a crossing there. If we lived or worked together later in life there is a point at which the lines converge, travel together for a while and then separate. If we have just met, the lines join where they end. If we make this at the foot of a Tor or under a bridge or on the sand beneath a low cliff we can then rise above it and see the web that we have made, the rich and unique tapestry that we have woven together with our lives.

After Daedelus the craftsmen finished building the labyrinth, Minos imprisoned him and his son Icarus within it to keep its secret safe. So, ever a resourceful man, Daedelus made them wings out of feathers and wax and so began another story. They too chose to rise above the shadows. Sometimes the only way out is up.

Reflections on freedom

Meditation has never come easy for me but I persevere nevertheless albeit not as often as I would like. Sometimes I start to meditate and then find myself standing at the stove making a cup of tea and can't quite recall how I got from one to the other. Such is the tricky nature of the mind. Usually I meditate by counting my breaths. Often, a little way into the process, I will start reflecting on freedom and how to attain it through meditation. I might follow this train of thought for a good many minutes before I realize that I have stopped counting my breaths. Instead of meditating, I am thinking about meditating.

Freedom is encumbered by illusion. We think that we will find it here or find it there but wherever we go we take our chains with us. The truth is that freedom can only be found within the heart. When we have cut ourselves free from all the emotional bonds that hold us to the past and all the expectations that tie us to the future and release the child within to be fully in the present then suddenly we will manifest freedom in our outer lives. But until then a tantalizing glimpse is the best we can hope for.

On ancient European rocks and tombs, usually from the Bronze Age, we occasionally find labyrinth patterns. These simple designs begin with a line that enters the centre of the pattern and then weaves back and forth around it in ever increasing concentric circles with each sweep bringing it back into relationship with the centre until it leaves the pattern at the point where it began. Some have a number of possible pathways, some of which lead to dead ends. There are many possible interpretations of this but one that particularly interests me is that this may be a map of the journey of a human soul through a lifetime. We enter at the heart of ourselves in the place of the feminine, where the inner child stays for ever. The needs of our masculine take us out into the world where we put ever increasing distance between ourselves and that child. But the cycles of our lives bring us back, time and time again, back into relationship with the centre. As we grow we journey ever outwards, making our mark upon time like the ripples on a pond. Some of our pathways are fruitless and we have to turn around and start again. But always we are called home to ourselves until at last in the feminine of elder hood we return fully to our heart and leave from the point at which we began.

All children begin free. If we are lucky we may hold on to this freedom for most of our infancy, although from an early age those around us will be trying to tie us down. To watch a young child who has managed so far to avoid or resist this is a great lesson in freedom. They are completely present. They are free in their body, in their voice, in their creativity, in their feelings. They are spontaneous, they are joyous, they are powerful. It doesn't matter where they are; they take this freedom with them like a blessing. If a child is allowed to cultivate this freedom for all of their infancy, the first seven years of their life, they will have a foundation of freedom at the very heart of themselves. Unfortunately unconscious parenting, social expectations and academic pressures rarely allow this. Steiner education is an exception to the latter where children are kept in kindergarten until their school readiness is assessed at six and a half, after which reading and writing can begin.

Kindergarten. The children's garden. This is the Eden in which we begin, the garden of our own hearts. The longer we are allowed to stay there the better we will know that place within ourselves and the easier we will find it to return there. Because as parents we are only human and cannot be conscious all the time we will inevitably wound our children in some way and they will have to spend their lives healing this wound, just as we have. But the more we face and confront our own wounding and spare the children the legacy the more we allow them to keep the keys to the garden. We all fall from Grace; it is what makes us human. But we are all called back to ourselves as well and that is what sets us free.

The spiraling backwards and forwards of these ancient labyrinths also describes the passage of the year as it swings between the outward compulsion of the masculine and the inward draw of the feminine. Now as the year comes close to completion and we begin to head back to the point from which we began we begin to realize that we are about to leave the map. Only death is on the horizon.

But what may lie beyond that?

Chapter 12 October

Direction

October arrives and the days grow shorter and colder. The countryside is yellowing now and the leaves are beginning to crunch underfoot. The end of this cycle of growth is coming closer now and we feel in the crisp Autumnal air our potential for change, the promise of a new cycle soon to begin. But we feel death too, all around us and within.

Winter is beginning to stir and her first breath sows a chill into the night which lingers still when morning comes and reminds us of where we are heading. Some of the trees are already beginning to reveal their skeletal forms and views are opening up on hillsides where before only forest could be seen.

The last of the harvest is still being gathered. The sweet chestnuts line the forest pathways like an army of little hedgehogs waiting for inquisitive noses, insistent beaks or gentle and courageous fingers to tease them open. In the school yards the horse chestnuts are having their horsepower tested in conker fights, banging and cracking one against the other like the antlers of the great stags who are still rutting and roaring in the secret arenas of the dark woods. The smell of bonfires lingers on the autumn air while golden orange flashes, incandescent yellows and earthy, plummy reds begin to lick through the foliage of the trees like flames. The blackberries are done now but the rosehips, sloes, hazelnuts and haws are still sustaining the little souls that depend upon them. The meadows are dry and brown, a crisp and crunching melee of coarse stalks and seed heads. The green is being drained from the earth, slipping away little by little like an unfast dye.

As we walk through the forest and feel the old year dying around us we can look down and see the seeds of the year to come nestling once again among the fallen leaves. All must die, but in the heart of death we find the seeds of life waiting.

As we approach the new cycle we begin to sense the direction it will take us in. This may not be a direction we have chosen. A plant that the Celts associated with this time is the reed. Growing beside the flowing river, the reed symbolizes direction and in particular the direction of flow into which we are called. The reed feels the flow and moves with it for to resist is futile in the face of such compulsion. Struggles arise when we try to change this or attempt to swim against the current. When we drink from the cup of the feminine and listen to our hearts we know inherently in which direction the flow is leading us even though our minds may disagree or our fears keep us from it.

In the book of Exodus the Egyptian Pharaoh proclaimed that all Hebrew boy children should be thrown into the river at birth to cull the Hebrew population. A woman, who we know only as a daughter of Levi, gave birth to a son and fearing for his life hid him for three months until, unable to hide him any longer, she placed him in a basket of reeds among the bulrushes. Her sister watched over him from afar. When the Pharaoh's daughter found the baby and decided to keep him, the sister approached the princess to recommend a wet nurse. When the princess agreed, the child's mother was fetched and reunited with her baby. The Pharaoh's daughter named the child Moses and brought him up as her son.

The reed basket is a symbol of the feminine, the womb that holds the child within, helpless, vulnerable and feeling. The story begins with fear, the hiding of the child. October often begins this way. We sense the direction of the river but see only the perils and we dare not risk our soft and vulnerable selves in this change. But in the end we have no choice because Pharaoh, the higher manifesting self, is throwing the new life into the current and making the old way increasingly difficult to sustain. The leaves are dying and they can only cling on for so long. Then the old year must fall. In the end we have only our trust to rely on and the month of October is a gathering time for trust. When we trust enough we will lay the child down beside the river and wait.

In that single act of trust Moses went from being born into a family of persecuted refugees to becoming a prince. We too are invited to ascend to a new level of being, a new cycle of growth. We are not abandoning our inner child; we are simply trusting enough to lay it down and then watching over it from afar. In the hope that it will be gathered up by royal hands and come into the fullness of its promise.

We often make images of our inner child at this time and place them into little baskets made from reed, dried grasses, clay, sticks, feathers and moss. We keep them safe and close while we acknowledge and honour our fears for the future. Then when we are ready we take them to the riverside and lay them down.

The reed basket is an image of the feminine because it is a container. The feminine is not a thing; it is that which contains the thing and what it contains is feeling. We think of it as the heart or the womb or as Nature. It has many symbols, the Holy Grail being just one of them. As the cup that Christ drank from at the last supper it grew to symbolize the feminine heart of Christ. As the church became increasingly patriarchal and repressed the Goddess in all her aspects, the quest for the grail became the search for the lost and sacred feminine, the feeling body of the divine self. In the story of Parsifal the knight heals the Fisher king and all his lands by simply asking the two questions in the grail castle: "what ails thee my lord?" and "whom does the grail serve?" These questions are so powerful because they address the problem and its cause. Here in the West we are very good at asking the first question because we are so comfortable with the masculine but the second question to the feminine often goes unasked. So we meet ill health, albeit physical, mental, sociological or ecological by treating the symptoms without considering the feeling causation that lies beneath. When we explore this in the magical language of metaphor the truth unfolds and nothing is as healing as the heart's truth.

Just as Moses led his people from bondage so these two mysterious questions offer us the promise of freedom. If we sit among the reeds on a river bank we may be lucky enough to see the fisher king released. Of all birds the kingfisher is most prone to soil his own nest and there is something very human in this, in the lives of struggle and shadow that we tend to manifest for ourselves. But released upon the water he is a streak of blue lightning, an angel, a dragon, a king.

The ship of renewal

Boats commonly figure in myths of dissolution and regeneration. The Babylonian ship of renewal carried the seeds of the new world down into the underworld where they lay dormant until the world began again. This is reminiscent of the night voyage of the Egyptian sun god Ra who every night sailed his solar barque through the deepest regions of the underworld to re-emerge again in the morning.

Flood myths occur all over the world and the story of Noah's ark has its roots in much older tales. In the Babylonian epic of Atrahasis humanity had multiplied so rapidly that their noise disturbed the god's peace. The god Enlil tried to reduce their numbers by sending plagues and droughts but each time the god of wisdom Enki intervened and revealed Enlil's intentions to Atrahasis the king. Atrahasis was then able to take counter measures to protect his people. Finally Enlil sent a flood but he bound the other gods with an oath of secrecy. Enki got around this by speaking not to the king but to the hut of reeds in which the king sat in retreat. Atrahasis heeded the warning and built a boat in which he took refuge with his family and various animals. After seven days the flood subsided and Atrahasis emerged. He was rewarded with eternal life.

The receiving of wisdom through the walls of a reed hut is a symbolic reference to the association between the reed and wise council. It is to this council that we must listen now, the higher voice within that clings not to the old world but sees the potential in the new. This is the voice of the inner elder, the gift of wisdom.

Cultures the world over entertain myths of cosmic dissolution with catastrophic events sweeping away the old in preparation for the new. As the autumn gales and storms descend upon us we feel our fears and insecurities about these winds and waters of change. Living in these times of climate change we find ourselves faced with apocalyptic reports of earthquakes, floods and other natural disasters. Most of the ancient myths include a welling up of the waters and now as the ice caps melt it seems as if we can expect this once again.

But water is always a metaphor for feeling, so these myths speak of a return to the feminine. They tell us that she can only be repressed for so long, by our patriarchal culture, by the head silencing the heart, and then she must break her banks and flood. If we have taken wise council and learned to be in relationship with the feminine, to ride upon our grief rather than be drowned by it, then we will have our ship of renewal when we need it. The reaction of the Earth is in response to an untethered masculine that strips the forests and bases its unsustainable vision on the burning of fossil fuels. The rising of the waters marks a swinging back towards the heart, where the land is felt as part of self. In this vision every forest becomes a place of healing, a therapeutic space in which we reconnect to our essential selves. Once we have so joined our hearts to the land we could no more hurt it than we could wound those that we love. In this vision all natural places are sacred.

This is the time when we make our own ships of renewal. Sometimes we make these out of clay and other natural materials: proud Viking long boats with serpent headed prows, little grassy coracles with mossy blankets to nestle under, rafts made from woven sticks with billowing dock leaf sails. But every year we also go in an ever increasing group to the estuary, where the river meets the sea, to make reed boats. First we choose a stone on the beach and naming what it is that we have to let go of first, something that is dying for us now, we throw it into the sea. Then tying bundles of reeds together we assemble them into little ships, each one unique, and place within them tokens of the wishes and affirmations that we are making for the cycle to come. We make these on the beach and then lay them in a line to admire them and share the meaning of our cargo. Then we name our little vessels, take them down to the river and set them free.

Working by the river we will probably disturb a heron. As they fly they usually fold their legs beneath them, unlike their cousins the cranes whose long legs hang and cross below them while their wings stretch out in a line on each side. Cranes make Ogham symbols in the air, and a poet of the Trojan War, Palamedes son of Nauplius (which means ancient intelligence, son of the navigator) was credited by the Greeks with having invented some of the Ogham letters, inspired by watching a flock of cranes fly by making letters as they flew. St Columba, who was trained in a Druid college, was known as the crane cleric because of his knowledge of Ogham. Herons and cranes are also living metaphors for direction and they point the way now, back to this ancient intelligence, this deep and inspired knowing that enables us to navigate through the mysteries of life and death.

The robe of the elder

A tree that the Celts associated with this time was the elder. Known as the witch's tree, the elder personifies the crone, the feminine as elder. The spirit of the elder is the Elder mother, also called Hyldemoer in Scandinavian myth, and she is a spirit of wisdom and earth magic. Known as the tree of regeneration because it can re-grow damaged branches and root from any part of itself, the elder speaks to us of the end in the beginning and the beginning in the end.

Elders are hunched, twisted and wizened trees and were often associated with witches. It was believed that some women could turn into elder trees and if you cut the tree the woman would bare the wound when she returned. So the elder represents the year as crone, the feminine grown old and wise and powerful. There was much fear and suspicion associated with this archetype and yet in pre Christian times these grandmothers were the source of wisdom and teaching for whole communities. In this time of death and dissolution it is to this elder within ourselves that we turn for wise council.

So elder marks the passage from the ending of things to their beginning. Elder shaped leaf images were used in megalithic burial mounds to protect and guide the departed spirits, while elder blossoms were used to bring good fortune to an unborn child and young mothers would kiss elder trees to ensure a safe and protected birth. Elder, the wise old crone of the year, lays us to rest and then acts as midwife at our rebirth. She helps us to let go of the old cycle, the old securities and expectations, the old hopes and dreams that are proving contrary to the flow of our life's great river. She helps us submit to this flow and let it carry us where it will, down into the darkness of the winter and through to a new beginning.

Because it is in the nature of our culture to neglect and malign the feminine in all its guises our elders often get a raw deal. Our obsession with youth and beauty leaves little room for the grace, wisdom and character of old age. In valuing only the qualities of the masculine: productivity, status and physical power, we condemn our elders to be treated as burdens, both by themselves and by their loved ones. Old age may become a place of scarce hope and promise, where the care home beckons and the world carries on without us.

But when we abandon our elders we abandon something vital within ourselves. Within the family the elder has a rightful place. This is the place of stillness, of presence and contemplation, of watching and holding, of deep knowing fed by experience. They are the storyteller, the bearer of the family's history, its rituals and its secrets. The robe that they wear has been woven from all the love, laughter, sacrifices and losses that they have known and shared with others. When we lose our elders this robe is lost too, and with it the soul of the family. Our children are raised without the grace and presence of elders to hold and guide them. As we pass mid life and grow old ourselves we have no healthy role models. We cannot take on the robe of the elder and so we may grow childlike, impotent and foolish instead, trying to act young despite our age because we believe that only youth has value.

But when we reclaim and honour our elders we reclaim and honour ourselves. When we sit with an elder and honour them rarely do we find ourselves compelled to list their achievements like a curriculum vitae. Rather, we honour them for the love that they have held and shared. For the sacrifices that they have made for love, for the dreams that they have realized and for the dreams that they had to forgo. For the times of loss and letting go and for the times that they clung on against all odds. For the choices that they made and for the things that they had no choice in. When we honour our elders in this way we give them that most precious of gifts, a sense of completion, and we give ourselves the realization that we too can be honoured for these things. No-one has learned the lessons of our lives as we have. Lessons in love, lessons in loss, lessons in courage, lessons in grief, lessons in struggle, lessons in freedom. Only we can eat the fruit of this tree because this tree is uniquely ours, as is the wisdom that it gives us. Now is the time to honour this.

The honouring of the elder within ourselves is a beautiful ritual that we share at this time. Working outdoors in a group we decorate a chair with sprays of elder. Then we find gifts for the others in the group, Nature's gifts to represents qualities that we wish to honour in each of them. One by one we sit in the chair and the robe of the elder is placed upon our shoulders. The others in the group honour us with their gifts and then we are asked for our own words of honouring, words of truth that declare the qualities that we respect in ourselves. Regardless of our age we are all elders of our own lives and of the cycle that is closing now. Our elder hood comes not from what we have done but from what we have felt, from the lessons that life has taught us and continues to teach us. In this respect even a child can honour the elder within themselves.

Others too. Honouring is a gift that we can give to even the most dishonoured. In a world that respects only achievement there are many that live with a perpetual sense of shame, disempowerment and failure. But regardless of whether we live in prison, in a mental hospital, in a night shelter or in a care home, we too are eating from the Tree of life and can honour the lessons that we have learned. We too can be honoured by others for the feeling qualities that they see in us. We too can accept the robe of the elder.

The dead time

As the ancient festival of Samhain approaches the year has grown old around and within us and we honour her death. The last few days of

October, leading up to Samhain, were considered to be the dead time, an empty space in which we wait between the old cycle and the new. This little pocket of time was like a thirteenth month, seemingly small yet connecting us to the infinite and eternal kingdom of the dead, the freedom and spaciousness that transcends all the cycles of life. At this time it was said that the veil between the living and the dead was thinnest and we could commune with our ancestors. Samhain itself was marked by a great fire festival and this event celebrated the beginning and ending of the year and was a time to honour our elders, both alive and dead. Known also as Halloween, or the holy evening, it was the most sacred time of the year. It is here that the elder tree really comes into its power.

It was believed that the elder mother could cure all the ills of mankind and village healers and herbalists would treat almost any ailment with its roots, leaves, flowers, bark and fruit. These old witches were the healers, shamans, midwives and wise women of the community and they held the wisdom and power of the feminine in their hearts. They were the living repositories of the stories, spells, metaphors and medicines that bound the people and their natural environment together. They had eaten the fruit of the Tree of life and now they shared its riches with others and were honoured as elders for doing so. But when the Christian authorities imposed their values upon the people they denounced the teachings of these elder mothers and gave the word witch a new meaning. The fire festival was moved away from Halloween and is now celebrated a week later and Halloween was demonized and used to frighten the populace with tales of ghosts, ghouls and malevolent hags. There began a great persecution of women in which millions were tortured and murdered for their faith and their knowledge, or at the whim of others. Not only did these centuries mark the loss of our relationship with the feminine and its inherent power and wisdom, but also the loss of our relationship with death and our ancestors. Death became a fearful thing, a place of judgement in which the threat of the fires of Hell was used to control and subjugate the living. The dead became nameless, ghostly, malevolent and clinging.

But who are the dead that stand so close to us now? They are those who were children, lovers, parents and elders before us. They are our own parents, grandparents and beloved elders who loved and guided us while they were alive and do so still. As our ancestors they were the foundation of our being, the soil in which we have grown. They were the leaves that fell so that the seeds of our lives would have riches to grow in. Samhain invites us to honour them as elders, for all they have given us. Not to fear them, but to celebrate their lives and their legacies.

We honour them because they are not forgotten. They ate the fruit of the tree of life and now they live forever. This is because every moment of their lives is set upon the body of time like the meandering trails of insects on the body of a tree. Every loving embrace, each and every fallen tear, the sparkling eyes and the beaming smile, the head held in the hands in despair, the raised voice in anger, the flowering of hope in the darkest place, the shocking revelation of truth, the blaze of power and the act of kindness, the surrendering to grace and the times of letting go, all of these and so much more remain exactly where they belong, in the everlasting moment in which they occurred. Nothing can take this away, not even time.

This is true of all death. When something or someone we have loved, be it a person, a relationship, a role, a place, a journey or a phase of our life passes beyond our reach it is vital that we grieve its passing for in the release of tears is the process of letting go. But beyond this comes the realization that nothing really dies. It may pass beyond us in the here and now but it stays always where it belongs and so stays always a part of us. From the place of elder hood we can look back upon our lives and touch these precious moments again with our hearts.

When my son turned eighteen we led him blindfolded out onto the moor and lay him down on the grassy mound of a Celtic burial chamber, where once a chieftain had been laid to rest. We covered him with a blanket and placed sprigs of heather all over him. Then we talked to the spirit of the boy who was passing. We talked of our love and of our grief. We acknowledged our clinging, our longing to keep the child with us and our knowledge that we must let go. We remembered stories of our times together. We cried. We sung to the boy one last time. Then we let him go.

After a little while we summoned the man and invited him to rise up from the boy's grave and meet us. We embraced him, released from our grief, relishing his manhood. Then we sat together on a Tor with the endless moor spreading out around us like an ocean of stone and enjoyed our new beginning.

To be in the presence of death is a great lesson in life. The word compassion means to be with the passion, as in the passion of Christ. It means to be with suffering. Not to try and fix or prevent it but simply to be there with an open heart and face with courage whatever comes.

Whether this means holding the hand of a loved one as they die or being with our own suffering as a child leaves home or a relationship ends, it is all the same. Endings come and they are hard. It helps to meet them with compassion.

A circle of trees

Standing on the threshold of death we can never know what lies beyond but we can turn around and see where we have come from. Do you remember the new beginnings of silver birch, the descent of rowan, the bridge of alder, the womb of willow, the alchemy of ash, the white track of hawthorn, the doorway of oak, the fire of holly, the dark pool of hazel, the harvest of apple, the block of ivy, the robe of elder? Each month has offered us the Tree of life in a different guise, twelve different faces of wisdom shaped by the season into metaphors that are meaningful to us then and only then. Learn about any one of these outside of their month and we may grasp a little with our mind but that is all. But feel our way into any one of these in their rightful time and the depth of the lesson can be profound and transformative for this is a teaching of the heart so the mind can only truly understand it when it has been felt in context with the turning year.

Environmental arts therapy provides the perfect vehicle for this teaching because the moment we walk into the woods we are in context. We cannot but feel our place in the cycle because it is all around us and within us too. The metaphors that we have talked about here are not imposed upon people, they occur naturally and spontaneously in everyone's work, in one form or another, regardless of whether the individual is aware of them or not. They are perhaps archetypal, or at least they are cultural, shaped by our history, our traditions and our seasons. No doubt in another culture and another climate there will be other trees, other metaphors. But there will always be twelve months, twelve unique and unfolding lessons. Having knowledge of them before hand allows the therapist to find new pathways through old problems that others might miss, to become a navigator in the vast and watery realm of feeling. Sharing that knowledge with people fosters a deep sense of reconnection, a remembering of something profound and vital within ourselves, our true and beloved home, our very human nature. Once we have integrated that knowledge we have a practice for life as year after year we spiral deeper into relationship with ourselves.

Imagine yourself now standing in the centre of this circle. Each tree, each with its own unique character offers up its gifts to you now. Imagine the circle becoming smaller as the trees close in and become part of you. Imagine them becoming one single tree, growing at the heart of your being. This is the Tree of life and its fruit is always there for the taking. Eat me, it says.

Every time we eat we grow wiser. We see that even though the metaphors that enable the process are unique to every month, the process is always fundamentally the same. We seek the child. We empower the masculine to release the feminine. We manifest change.

The circle of trees does not just teach us about the turning year but about the cycles of a human life as well and it is true once again that only when we are living each cycle can we truly know it. So the gift of elder hood is the culmination of a lifetime's lessons in what it means to be human. Often it is only at the end that we really understand the magnitude of what we have learned. In the book of Revelation, in the very last chapter of the Bible, we read:

"And he shewed me a pure river of water of life, clear as a crystal, proceeding out of the throne of God and of the Lamb. In the midst of the street of it, and on either side of the river, was there the Tree of life, which bare twelve manner of fruits, and yielded her fruit every month: and the leaves of the tree were for the healing of the nations."

So once again, we are not learning something new; we are just remembering something that many of us have long forgotten. Is it not true that the healing of the nations begins with the healing of the self? Imagine the difference that one generation of courageous adults who were willing to face and address their own wounds rather than passing the legacy down to their children could make. As long as we continue to hide from the feminine we will be forced into ever darker regions of the masculine and we will neglect and abuse our world and those among us who are vulnerable in ever more damaging ways. But as soon as we begin to embrace, defend, honour and release the feminine everything changes. Every single one of us, however insignificant we may feel, has a part to play in this extraordinary, all encompassing story of descent, redemption and renewal.

The sea

All rivers, even the river of the water of life, lead down to the sea. Manannan, the Celtic god of the sea, possessed a bag made from the skin of the crane in which he kept his most magical possessions, each a metaphor for a letter of the Ogham alphabet. So it is perhaps not surprising that the final letter in this alphabet is his own, Mor, the sea.

If water is a metaphor for feeling then the sea is the heart of all. It is both the beginning and the ending of the circle. When we watch the cycle of the waters turning we can see all but its beginning. The clouds we can see, the rain we can see, the rivers we can see, the estuaries we can see and the ocean we can see. But the rising of the vapour from the surface of the ocean is invisible to us.

Is death not the same as this? Is death not the great sea from which we emerge and into which we return? If we consider that infants and elders are human beings at their most feminine then does this not suggest that death is the feminine in its purest state? All being. All feeling. No doing. If this is so then the dead are perhaps more present then we can ever imagine. Is it also not so that we can see every part of the cycle of life but its beginning? We can see the child, the adolescent, the adult, the elder and the dead. But the rising of the spirit from the surface of death and its return to the cycle is invisible to us.

If death is the great heart of all then we are fools to fear it so. For at the heart of all feeling is love. There is no anger, no sadness, no guilt and no fear, that does not hold at its core this most sublime of all human emotions. So if death is the pure feminine then surely death is a state of infinite and eternal love. Again and again, it might appear, we are scooped up from this still and silent place and cast upon the hillsides to wend our way down through every possible obstacle, trial and test that might be conceived of. But it is from love that we come and it is to love that we return and in our heart of hearts we never lose our connection to this great and everlasting ocean.

In the story of the Selkie a lonely young fisherman comes across seven beautiful maidens dancing naked on the sand. Beside them on a rock were a pile of discarded seal skins. Silently he crept up and took one. At that moment the girls cried out and all but one ran to the rock, gathered up their skins, put them back on and slipped into the sea. Only one beautiful girl remained, with eyes like a seal, and she stood before him and asked for her skin back. "Come with me" he said "and I will find new clothes for you". So the fisherman and the Selkie were married and she bore him a son and a daughter. They lived a simple life and a hard one but they loved each other. Still the woman never forgot her true home and sometimes when weaving by candle light she would gently sway and sing the songs of the ocean to her children. Then one day when her children were almost grown her daughter, while digging in the field, found a pelt of soft and shining skin that had been buried there. She brought it to her mother who held it to her heart and wept with sadness and relief. Then the woman told her children that she must leave them, that she would always love them but that she must return to the sea from whence she came. She put her seal skin back on and slipped away beneath the waves. They never saw her again.

Each of us is born from the waters and loses the caul, the skin in which we come. We are given new clothes, new roles, new loves and new struggles but the feminine within never forgets the great ocean from which she has been borne. Like the fisherman, our masculine strives to make us a good home in this life. But the feminine is a child of the great heart, that ocean that transcends the cycles of life, infinite, eternal, beloved. We do the best we can, under the circumstances. But when the time comes we put back on the skin, become now the robe of the elder, and saying our goodbyes to those that we have loved, we slip away.

There is a beautiful ceremony called the grieving tree that we can use to honour those that have slipped away from us. Choose a tree that in your opinion best defines the one who has gone, perhaps an oak for strength and endurance, a hazel for creativity and intuition, an elder for wisdom and elderhood or a rowan for magic and protection. Choose a location that suits the tree, somewhere it will thrive. Invite only those that loved the beloved, this is not a ceremony for casual acquaintances or curious spectators. Now invite everyone to make a totem of their love from the natural materials around them. Together plant the tree and then take turns to place your totem among the branches or around its roots and as you do so speak aloud to the spirit of the one you have lost. It is this honouring of the dead in the first person, as if face to face, that allows grief to flow. Your tears are the greatest gift of love that you can give at this time. When we cry together in this way we accept also their gift to us: the cementing together of our community with love, honesty and truth, shared now in reaction to their passing. We teach our children and remind ourselves that love is at the heart of death and that there is nothing to fear but our tears, and our tears release us back into life.

So for now, the cycle is ending. Once again the hillsides burst into colour and smoulder in the low autumn sunshine like the outspread wings of the Phoenix. It is good to wrap ourselves up warm against the cold and walk through the whirling leaves, to feel the crunch of the old year underneath our feet and know that nothing ever really ends, for as we breathe out our last breath in one reality we prepare to breathe in our first in the next. Here once again we can gather our seeds. Seeds of hope, seeds of renewal, new dreams and new beginnings.

Down by the water's edge, our ship awaits.

About the author

Ian Siddons Heginworth lives with his wife and children in Exeter, Devon. He is a leading practitioner, innovator and teacher of environmental arts therapy, a practical ecopsychology that uses the locations, themes, cycles and materials of Nature as its therapeutic media. He is a drama therapist registered with the U.K. Health Professions Council and has an Mphil in drama. He is employed by Devon Partnership Trust as a specialist practitioner, running the Wild Things project, which combines environmental arts therapy with outward bound activities, for mental health service users in Exeter. He is also employed as a lecturer and workshop leader on the Exeter based M.A. in drama therapy course. As the founder of Dreamtime Theatre he has led many large community arts workshops, performances and rituals in outdoor locations throughout the U.K and in the U.S. He has worked as a therapist for over twenty years and runs a private practice as an environmental arts therapist in therapeutic woodland around Exeter.

Inspiration

These are the books that helped to inform and inspire this writing:

Jacqueline Memory Paterson, Tree wisdom, The definitive guidebook to the myth, folklore and healing power of trees, Thorsons, 1996

Liz and Colin Murray, The Celtic Tree Oracle, A system of divination, Connections book publishing 1998

Theodore Roszak, Mary E. Gomes, Allen D. Kanner (Editors) Ecopsychology, Restoring the Earth, Healing the mind, Sierra club books,1995

Glennie Kindred, The Tree Ogham, published by the author, 1997

Glennie Kindred, The Sacred Tree, published by the author, 1995

T.W.Rolleston, Celtic myths and legends, Senate, 1994

Roger Cook, The tree of life, Avon books, 1974

Ann Druitt, Christine Fynes-Clinton and Marije Rowling, All year round, Hawthorn Press, 1995

Diana Carey and Judy Large, Festivals, family and food, Guide to seasonal celebration, Hawthorn Press, 1982

Post Wheeler (forward), Russian Fairy tales, Senate 1995

Robert Bly, A little book on the human shadow, Harper San Francisco, 1988

Robert Bly, Iron John, A book about men, Element, 1990

Clarrissa Pinkola Estes, Women who run with the wolves, Rider 1992

Edmond Bordeaux Szekely (translater), The Gospel of the Essenes, The C.W.Daniel Co.Ltd 1937

Jay Ramsay, Alchemy, The art of transformation, Thorsons, 1997

Alexander Roob, Alchemy and mysticism, Taschen, 1996

Steve Biddulph, Manhood, Finch publishing, 1994

Padraic Colum, The story of King Arthur and other Celtic heroes, Dover, 2005

Winnifred Gallagher, The power of place, Harper Perennial, 1994

Joseph Jacobs (Editor), Celtic Fairy tales, Senate, 1994

Stephen and Ondra Levine, Embracing the Beloved, Relationship as a path of awakening, Gateway books, 1996

Jacob and Wilhelm Grimm, Selected tales, Penguin books, 1982

Jean Giono, The man who planted trees, Peter Owen, 1989

Robert Graves, The Greek myths, Penguin books, 1992

Jeffrey Gantz (translator) Early Irish myths and sagas, Penguin books, 1981

Patrick White, The tree of man, Penguin books, 1956

Dorothy L.Sayers (translator) The comedy of Dante Alighieri the Florentine, Penguin books 1955

Connie Zweig and Steve Wolf, Romancing the shadow, Ballantine books, 1997

The Holy Bible, Authorized King James edition

I would especially like to thank all the people who I have worked with in environmental arts therapy over the years. Your powerful and beautiful work, your honesty, courage and insights lie like a foundation beneath everything in this book and it has always been such a privilege to walk with you into the shadows and discover together the wonders that await us there .

Lightning Source UK Ltd.
Milton Keynes UK
UKHW01f0053060918
328392UK00001B/152/P